T0089141

"As Carl Rogers taught, 'That which is most personal is most general.' These beautiful stories uniformly teach most of us at the personal level. They uplift and inspire and entertain and edify. As I love good quotation books, I love this book of stories."

Dr. Stephen R. Covey
Author, 7 Habits of Highly Effective People

"Any 'medicine' that has side effects should have a warning label, and these *Chicken Soup* books are no exception. People who read them should be cautioned . . .

> 'WARNING—Reading this book will probably cause laughter, tears, lumps in the throat and a permanent increase in love, courage and personal responsibility.'

Jim Newman, CPAE
Author, Release Your Brakes!

"You can never get too much chicken soup, at least that's what Mom always said. This second helping of *Chicken Soup for the Soul* is the kind of medicine that goes down easily . . . and leaves a warm and memorable feeling all day long."

Harvey Mackay
Author, Swim with the Sharks Without Being Eaten Alive

"Jack Canfield and Mark Victor Hansen's collection of stories in *Soup* has a wonderful blend of wisdom and insight, just a dash of foolishness and smiles, much more than a pinch of kindness, with enough warmth to light the corners of the gloomiest of hearts. It's great fireside fare for folks who are happy, troubled, disheartened, sick, or anyone who watches "Court TV." It's nutritious for the soul and good for you. Try it twice each day and call me in the morning!"

Steve Allen, Jr., M.D.
Humorist, Author and Associate Dean for Student Affairs for the College of Medicine at the Health Science Center in Syracuse, NY.

"This book is a deliciously enjoyable treat that takes you above the petty into the world of light, love . . . and possibility."

Susan Jeffers, Ph.D.
Author, Feel the Fear and Do It Anyway *and* Dare to Connect

"With *A 2nd Helping* . . . Mark Victor Hansen and Jack Canfield have struck gold again. There's real take-home value in this one. I give it another perfect 10!"

Peter Vidmar
Olympic Gold Medalist in Gymnastics

"Wonderful book . . . whenever I need a boost I take a 'second helping.' It warms my heart and lifts my spirits."

Robert Kriegel
Author, If It Ain't Broke . . . Break It!

"Hearts will be warmed and free spirit will soar for those who read Mark Victor Hansen and Jack Canfield's *Chicken Soup for the Soul.*"

Al Neuharth
Founder, USA Today

"Chicken Soup for the Soul is a priceless collection of powerful stories that will move you to look at your life anew. Each story broadens our perspective of what it means to be fully human and teaches us that greater love, courage and compassion can be part of our own story."

John Gray
Author, Men Are From Mars, Women Are from Venus *and* What Your Mother Couldn't Tell You and Your Father Didn't Know

"Jack Canfield and Mark Victor Hansen are two of the few good, outstanding, giving, loving people alive."

Larry Wilde
"America's bestselling humorist"—The New York Times

A 2nd Helping of
CHICKEN SOUP
FOR THE SOUL®

A 2nd Helping of Chicken Soup for the Soul
More Stories to Open the Heart and Rekindle the Spirit
Jack Canfield, Mark Victor Hansen

Published by Backlist, LLC,
a unit of Chicken Soup for the Soul Publishing, LLC. www.chickensoup.com

Copyright ©2012 by Chicken Soup for the Soul Publishing, LLC.
All Rights Reserved.

No part of this publication may be reproduced, stored in a retrieval system or
transmitted in any form or by any means, electronic, mechanical, photocopying,
recording or otherwise, without the written permission of the publisher.

CSS, Chicken Soup for the Soul, and its Logo and Marks are trademarks of
Chicken Soup for the Soul Publishing LLC.

Front cover redesign by Lawna P. Oldfield
Originally published in 1995 by Health Communications, Inc.

Back cover and spine redesign by Pneuma Books, LLC

Distributed to the booktrade by Simon & Schuster. SAN: 200-2442

Publisher's Cataloging-in-Publication Data
(Prepared by The Donohue Group)

A 2nd helping of chicken soup for the soul : more stories to open the heart and
  rekindle the spirit / [compiled by] Jack Canfield [and] Mark Victor Hansen.
   p. : ill. ; cm.

  Originally published: Deerfield Beach, FL : Health Communications, c1995.
ISBN: 978-1-62361-035-7
  1. Spiritual life--Anecdotes. 2. Anecdotes. I. Canfield, Jack, 1944- II. Hansen,
Mark Victor. III. Title: Second helping of chicken soup for the soul IV. Title:
Chicken soup for the soul

BL624 .A12 2012
158/.12   2012913037

PRINTED IN THE UNITED STATES OF AMERICA
on acid free paper

22 21 20 19 18 17 16 15 14 13   01 02 03 04 05 06 07 08 09 10

A 2nd Helping of
CHICKEN SOUP FOR THE SOUL®

More **Stories To Open The Heart And Rekindle The Spirit**

Jack Canfield
and
Mark Victor Hansen

CSS

Backlist, LLC, a unit of
Chicken Soup for the Soul Publishing, LLC
Cos Cob, CT
www.chickensoup.com

Contents

1. ON LOVE

2. ON PARENTING

3. ON DEATH AND DYING

4. A MATTER OF ATTITUDE

5. ON LEARNING AND TEACHING

6. LIVE YOUR DREAM

7. OVERCOMING OBSTACLES

8. ECLECTIC WISDOM

Dear Reader

I am here for you. When you are lonely or feel isolated, seek my companionship. When you are filled with doubt and your self-confidence seems to be a distant memory, look to my light. When confusion and chaos appear to reign supreme in your life, listen to my wisdom. As your grandparents used chicken soup to restore health to your body, I am here to give life to your soul. My insights into family and love will guide you out of the caverns of your solitude. My stories of courage and fortitude will strengthen your resolve.

My recipe contains a strong dose of inspiration offered by those who have faced mountains of challenge, only to overcome and stand above them among the clouds and stars. Your entire system will vibrate with new energy and lightness as you consume large quantities of humor, as you struggle to share your gifts with a world in need. Tales of the champions, the heroes and the heroines who have gone before you, will give new energy to your step and vitality to your dreams. Great thoughts uttered by the wisest of souls will break the shackles of fear that hold you in bondage.

Above all, I offer you the vitamin of vision—the vision of your future filled with joy, victory, happiness, health, prosperity, companionship and love. I am *Chicken Soup for the Soul*.

John Wayne Schlatter

Introduction

The universe is made of stories, not of atoms.

Muriel Ruckeyser

From our hearts to yours, we are delighted to offer you *A 2nd Helping of Chicken Soup for the Soul.* This book contains stories that we believe will inspire and motivate you to love more unconditionally, live with more passion and pursue your heartfelt dreams with more conviction. It will sustain you in times of frustration and failure and comfort you in times of pain and loss. It will become a lifetime companion offering support and wisdom whenever you need it.

You are about to embark on a wonderful journey. This book is different from other books you have read. At times it will touch you at the depths of your being. At other times it will transport you to new levels of love and joy. Our first *Chicken Soup for the Soul* book was so powerful that nonreaders reported that they read the entire book cover to cover. We wondered how this could be possible. They told us that the love energy, the inspiration and the tears and cheers for their soul captivated them and motivated them to read on.

I am only ten and I love this book. It's amazing that I love this book. I used not to read, but now I read, read and read.

Ryan O.—4th grade

How to Read This Book

This book could be read all at once in one sitting; however, we don't recommend it. We suggest that you slow down, take your time, savor it like a fine wine—one sip at a time. Each little sip will give you a warm glow, a tingling spirit and a radiant countenance. You will find that each story will nourish your heart, mind and soul in a different way. We invite you to surrender to the process and to give yourself enough time to digest each story. If you rush through them, you may miss the deeper meanings that lie beneath the surface. Each story contains a great deal of life wisdom and experience.

Having received thousands of letters from readers describing how the book affected their lives, we are more convinced than ever that stories are one of the most potent tools we can use to transform our lives. Stories speak directly to our subconscious mind. They lay down blueprints for living a better life. They offer practical solutions to our everyday problems and model creative behavior that works. They heal our wounds and remind us of the grandest aspects of our nature. They lift us out of our habitual day-to-day lives and awaken us to infinite possibilities. They inspire us to do and be more than we originally thought possible.

Share These Stories with Others

You may have tangible wealth untold,
Caskets of jewels and coffers of gold.

Richer than I you could never be;
I know someone who told stories to me.
                              Cynthia Pearl Maus

Some of the stories you read will move you to share them with a loved one or a friend. When a story really touches you to the depths of your soul, close your eyes ever so briefly and ask yourself, "Who needs to hear this story right now?" Someone you care about may come to mind. Take the time to go to them or call them and share the story with them. You will get something even deeper for yourself from sharing the story with someone you care about. Consider the following from Martin Buber:

> *A story must be told in such a way that it consti-*
> *tutes help in itself. My grandfather was lame.*
> *Once they asked him to tell a story about his*
> *teacher. And he related how his teacher used to hop*
> *and dance while he prayed. My grandfather rose as*
> *he spoke, and he was so swept away by his story*
> *that he began to hop and dance and show how the*
> *master had done. From that hour on he was cured*
> *of his lameness. That's how to tell a story!*

Consider sharing these stories at work, at church, synagogue or temple, and at home with your family. After sharing, discuss how the story affected you and why you were drawn to share it with them. And most important, let these stories inspire you to share your own stories.

Reading about, telling and listening to each others' stories can be very transformational. Stories are powerful vehicles that release our unconscious energies to heal, to integrate, to express and to grow. Hundreds of readers have told us about how the first book of Chicken Soup stories opened a floodgate of human emotions and facilitated deep family and group sharings. Family members started recalling and relating important experiences in their lives and began to bring those to the dinner table, the family meeting, the classroom, the support group, the church fellowship and even the workplace.

> *One of the most valuable things we can do to heal one another is listen to each other's stories.*
> *Rebecca Falls*

One teacher in Pennsylvania had her fifth-grade class collaborate to write their own *Chicken Soup for the Soul* book with moving stories from their own lives. Once the book was written and compiled, it was duplicated and circulated. It had a profound impact on both the students and their parents.

A manager at a Fortune 500 company told us she has started every staff meeting for a year with a story from *Chicken Soup for the Soul.*

Ministers, rabbis, psychologists, counselors, trainers and support group leaders have been beginning and ending their sermons and their sessions with stories from the book. We encourage you to do this too. People are hungry for this nurturance for the soul. It takes so little time and can have such a lasting impact.

We also encourage you to begin telling your stories to those around you. People may need to hear your story. As several stories in this book will point out, it may even save someone's life.

> *Sometimes our light goes out but is blown into flame by another human being. Each of us owes deepest thanks to those who have rekindled this light.*
> *Albert Schweitzer*

There have been many people who have rekindled our lights over the years, and we are grateful to them. We hope that, in some small way, we will be part of rekindling your light and blowing it into a bigger flame. If we do, then we have been successful.

Jack Canfield and Mark Victor Hansen

1

ON LOVE

Life is a song—sing it.
Life is a game—play it.
Life is a challenge—meet it.
Life is a dream—realize it.
Life is a sacrifice—offer it.
Life is love—enjoy it.

Sai Baba

CALVIN AND HOBBES© Watterson. Reprinted with permission of Universal Press Syndicate.
All rights reserved.

The Circus

That best portion of a good man's life,
His little, nameless, unremembered acts
Of kindness and of love.

William Wordsworth

Once when I was a teenager, my father and I were standing in line to buy tickets for the circus. Finally, there was only one family between us and the ticket counter. This family made a big impression on me. There were eight children, all probably under the age of 12. You could tell they didn't have a lot of money. Their clothes were not expensive, but they were clean. The children were well-behaved, all of them standing in line, two-by-two behind their parents, holding hands. They were excitedly jabbering about the clowns, elephants and other acts they would see that night. One could sense they had never been to the circus before. It promised to be a highlight of their young lives.

The father and mother were at the head of the pack standing proud as could be. The mother was holding her husband's hand, looking up at him as if to say, "You're my knight in shining armor." He was smiling and basking in pride, looking at her as if to reply, "You got that right."

The ticket lady asked the father how many tickets he wanted. He proudly responded, "Please let me buy eight children's tickets and two adult tickets so I can take my family to the circus."

The ticket lady quoted the price.

The man's wife let go of his hand, her head dropped, the man's lip began to quiver. The father leaned a little closer and asked, "How much did you say?"

The ticket lady again quoted the price.

The man didn't have enough money.

How was he supposed to turn and tell his eight kids that he didn't have enough money to take them to the circus?

Seeing what was going on, my dad put his hand into his pocket, pulled out a $20 bill and dropped it on the ground. (We were not wealthy in any sense of the word!) My father reached down, picked up the bill, tapped the man on the shoulder and said, "Excuse me, sir, this fell out of your pocket."

The man knew what was going on. He wasn't begging for a handout but certainly appreciated the help in a desperate, heartbreaking, embarrassing situation. He looked straight into my dad's eyes, took my dad's hand in both of his, squeezed tightly onto the $20 bill, and with his lip quivering and a tear streaming down his cheek, he replied, "Thank you, thank you, sir. This really means a lot to me and my family."

My father and I went back to our car and drove home. We didn't go to the circus that night, but we didn't go without.

Dan Clark

Shoes

As Gandhi stepped aboard a train one day, one of his shoes slipped off and landed on the track. He was unable to retrieve it as the train was moving. To the amazement of his companions, Gandhi calmly took off his other shoe and threw it back along the track to land close to the first. Asked by a fellow passenger why he did so, Gandhi smiled. "The poor man who finds the shoe lying on the track," he replied, "will now have a pair he can use."

Author Unknown
First quoted in *The Little, Brown Book of Anecdotes*

Chase

There was a definite quiver in Chase's lower lip as he followed his mother down the long, descending sidewalk to the parking lot at the orthodontist's office. This was going to be the worst summer of any that the 11-year-old boy had known. The doctor had been kind and gentle with him, but the time had come for him to face the reality that he would be fitted with braces to correct a misalignment of his teeth. The correction would hurt, he couldn't eat hard or chewy foods, and he thought he would be made fun of by his friends. No words passed between the mother and son as they drove back to the small, country home. It was only 17 acres, but it was a sanctuary for one dog, two cats, a rabbit and a multitude of squirrels and birds.

The decision to have Chase's teeth corrected had been a difficult one for his mother, Cindy. Having been divorced for five years, she was the sole provider for her young son. Little by little, she had saved up the $1,500 required to have the teeth corrected.

Then one sunny afternoon, the person she cared for the most, Chase, fell in love. Chase and his mother had gone to visit the Rakers, who were old family friends, at their farm about 50 miles away. Mr. Raker took them out to the barn and there she was. She held her head high as the trio approached. Her light mane and tail rippled on a gentle breeze. Her name was Lady, and she was everything a beautiful mare should be. She was saddled, and Chase had his first taste of horsemanship. There was an instant attraction, which seemed to be mutual.

"She is for sale, if you want to buy her," Mr. Raker had told Cindy. "For $1,500 you get the mare, all the papers on her and the horse trailer to haul her." For Cindy, it was a big decision. The $1,500 she had saved would fix Chase's teeth or buy Lady for Chase, but it wouldn't do both. Finally, she determined that getting the braces was the best long-term decision for Chase. It was a tearful decision for both mother and son. But Cindy promised to take Chase to the Raker farm to see Lady and ride her as often as they could.

Chase reluctantly began his long torturous course of treatment. With little courage and a low tolerance for pain, Chase submitted himself for the impressions, fittings and never-ending tightening of the expanders. He gagged, cried and pleaded, but the orthodontic correction went ahead. The only shining moments of Chase's life that summer came when his mother took him to ride Lady. There, he was free. Horse and rider would go galloping into the big pastures and into a world that knew no pain or suffering. There was only the steady rhythm of the horse's hooves on the sod and the wind in his face. Riding Lady, Chase could be John Wayne, "tall in the saddle," or one of the knights of old, off to rescue the fair maiden in distress, or anything his imagination let him be. At the end of his long rides, Chase and Mr. Raker would rub down Lady, clean her stall and feed her, and Chase would always give his new friend lumps of sugar. Cindy and Mrs. Raker spent their afternoons together making cookies and lemonade, and watching Chase ride his new best friend.

The goodbyes between Chase and the mare lasted as long as Cindy would permit. Chase would hold the horse's head in his hands, and then rub her strong shoulders and comb his fingers through her mane. The gentle animal seemed to understand the affection given to her and would stand patiently, now and then nipping at his shirt sleeve. Each time they left the Raker farm, Chase feared that this might be his last look at the mare. Lady was, after all, for sale, and the market was good for that quality of riding stock.

The summer wore on with repeated tightening of the expander in Chase's mouth. All of the discomfort would be worth it because this would make room for his yet undescended teeth to come in, he was told. Still, there was the agony of food particles trapped by the appliance, and that ever-constant pain of his facial bones stretching. All of the $1,500 would soon be used up on his dental work, and nothing would remain with which to purchase the mare he loved so much. Chase asked his mom countless questions, hoping for an answer that would eventually satisfy him. Could they borrow the money to buy the mare? Would Grandpa help them buy her? Could he get a job and save his money to buy the horse? His mother fielded the questions as best she could. And when all else failed, she would quietly slip away to shed her own tears, that she could not provide for all the wants of her only child.

A crisp September morning brought the opening of school, which also brought the big yellow school bus to the end of the lane at Chase's home. The schoolchildren took turns recounting the things they did during summer vacation. When his turn came, Chase talked about other subjects, but he never mentioned the golden-colored mare named Lady. The last chapter in that story had not yet been written, and he was afraid of how it would end. The battle with the stretching appliance in his mouth had been won, and the less obtrusive retainer had taken its place.

With eager anticipation, Chase looked forward to the third Saturday, when his mother had promised to take him to the Rakers' to ride Lady. Chase was up early on the appointed day. He fed his rabbits, dogs and cats, and even found time to rake leaves in the backyard. Before Chase and his mother left the house, he filled his jacket pocket with sugar cubes for the golden-maned mare, who he knew would be waiting for him. To Chase, it seemed an eternity before his mother turned the car off the main road and down the lane to the Raker farm. Anxiously, Chase strained his eyes for a glimpse of the mare that he loved so much. As they drew closer to the farm house and barns, he looked, but Lady was nowhere to be seen. Chase's pulse pounded as he looked expectantly for the horse trailer. It was not there. Both the trailer and horse were gone. His worst nightmare had become a reality. Someone had surely bought the horse, and he would never see her again.

Chase began to feel an emptiness in the pit of his stomach that he had never known before. They got out of the car and ran up to the front door of the house. No one answered the doorbell. Only the big collie, Daisy, was there with tail wagging to greet them. While his mother sadly looked on, Chase ran to the barn where the mare had been kept. Her stall was empty, and the saddle and blanket were also gone. With tears streaming down his cheeks, Chase returned to the car and got in. "I didn't even get to say goodbye, Mom," he whimpered.

On the drive back home, both Cindy and Chase sat quietly with their own thoughts. The wound of losing his friend would be slow to heal, and Chase only hoped that the mare would find a good home with someone to love and take care of her. She would be in his prayers, and he would never forget their carefree times together. Chase's head was bowed and his eyes closed as Cindy pulled into the driveway of their home. He did not see the red, shiny horse trailer by their barn, or Mr. Raker standing beside his blue pick-up truck. When Chase finally looked up, their car had stopped and Mr. Raker was opening Chase's door. "How much money have you got saved up, Chase?" he asked.

This could not be real. Chase rubbed his eyes in disbelief. "Seventeen dollars," he answered in a halting voice.

"That's just what I wanted for this mare and trailer," said a smiling Mr. Raker. The transaction that followed would have rivaled any on record for speed and brevity. In only moments, the new, proud owner was climbing into the saddle, astride his beloved mare. Horse and rider were soon out of sight around the barn, headed for the open pasture beyond.

Mr. Raker never explained his actions, other than to say, "This is the best I have felt in years!"

Bruce Carmichael

Rescue at Sea

Years ago, in a small fishing village in Holland, a young boy taught the world about the rewards of unselfish service. Because the entire village revolved around the fishing industry, a volunteer rescue team was needed in cases of emergency. One night the winds raged, the clouds burst and a gale force storm capsized a fishing boat at sea. Stranded and in trouble, the crew sent out the S.O.S. The captain of the rescue rowboat team sounded the alarm and the villagers assembled in the town square overlooking the bay. While the team launched their rowboat and fought their way through the wild waves, the villagers waited restlessly on the beach, holding lanterns to light the way back.

An hour later, the rescue boat reappeared through the fog and the cheering villagers ran to greet them. Falling exhausted on the sand, the volunteers reported that the rescue boat could not hold any more passengers and they had to leave one man behind. Even one more passenger would have surely capsized the rescue boat and all would have been lost.

Frantically, the captain called for another volunteer team to go after the lone survivor. Sixteen-year-old Hans stepped forward. His mother grabbed his arm, pleading, "Please don't go. Your father died in a shipwreck 10 years ago and your older brother, Paul, has been lost at sea for three weeks. Hans, you are all I have left."

Hans replied, "Mother, I have to go. What if everyone said, 'I can't go, let someone else do it'? Mother, this time I have to do my duty. When the call for service comes, we all need to take our turn and do our part." Hans kissed his mother, joined the team and disappeared into the night.

Another hour passed, which seemed to Hans' mother like an eternity. Finally, the rescue boat darted through the fog with Hans standing up in the bow. Cupping his hands, the captain called, "Did you find the lost man?" Barely able to contain himself, Hans excitedly yelled back, "Yes, we found him. Tell my mother it's my older brother, Paul!"

Dan Clark

A Life Worth Saving

A man risked his life by swimming through the treacherous riptide to save a youngster being swept out to sea. After the child recovered from the harrowing experience, he said to the man, "Thank you for saving my life."

The man looked into the boy's eyes and said, "That's okay, kid. Just make sure your life was worth saving."

Author Unknown
from More Sower's Seeds *by Brian Cavanaugh*

The Two-Hundredth Hug

*Love cures people—both the ones who give
it and the ones who receive it.*

Dr. Karl Menninger

My father's skin was jaundiced as he lay hooked up
to monitors and intravenous tubes in the intensive
care unit of the hospital. Normally a well-built man,
he had lost more than 30 pounds.

My father's illness had been diagnosed as cancer of
the pancreas, one of the most malignant forms of the
disease. The doctors were doing what they could but
told us that he had only three to six months to live.
Cancer of the pancreas does not lend itself to radiation therapy or chemotherapy, so they could offer little hope.

A few days later, when my father was sitting up in
bed, I approached him and said, "Dad, I feel deeply for
what's happened to you. It's helped me to look at the
ways I've kept my distance and to feel how much I
really love you." I leaned over to give him a hug, but
his shoulders and arms became tense.

"C'mon, Dad, I really want to give you a hug."

For a moment he looked shocked. Showing affection was not our usual way of relating. I asked him to

sit up some more so I could get my arms around him. Then I tried again. This time, however, he was even more tense. I could feel the old resentment starting to build up, and I began to think, "I don't need this. If you want to die and leave me with the same coldness as always, go right ahead."

For years I had used every instance of my father's resistance and rigidness to blame him, to resent him and to say to myself, "See, he doesn't care." This time, however, I thought again and realized the hug was for my benefit as well as my father's. I wanted to express how much I cared for him no matter how hard it was for him to let me in. My father had always been very Germanic and duty-oriented; in his childhood, his parents must have taught him how to shut off his feelings in order to be a man.

Letting go of my long-held desire to blame him for our distance, I was actually looking forward to the challenge of giving him more love. I said, "C'mon, Dad, put your arms around me."

I leaned up close to him at the edge of the bed with his arms around me. "Now squeeze. That's it. Now again, squeeze. Very good!"

In a sense I was showing my father how to hug, and as he squeezed, something happened. For an instant, a feeling of "I love you" bubbled through. For years our greeting had been a cold and formal handshake that said, "Hello, how are you?" Now, both he and I waited for that momentary closeness to happen again. Yet, just at the moment when he would begin to enjoy the feelings of love, something would tighten in his upper torso and our hug would become awkward and strange. It took months before his rigidness gave way and he was able to let the emotions inside him pass through his arms to encircle me.

It was up to me to be the source of many hugs

before my father initiated a hug on his own. I was not blaming him, but supporting him; after all, he was changing the habits of an entire lifetime—and that takes time. I knew we were succeeding because more and more we were relating out of care and affection. Around the two-hundredth hug, he spontaneously said out loud, for the first time I could ever recall, "I love you."

Harold H. Bloomfield, M.D.

A Strawberry Malt and Three Squeezes, Please!

My mother loved strawberry malts. It was always a thrill for me to drop in to see her and surprise her with her favorite refreshment.

In their later years, both my mom and dad lived in a life-care retirement center. Partially due to the stress of my mom's Alzheimer's condition, my dad became ill and was no longer able to care for her. They lived in separate rooms yet were together as much as they could be. They loved each other so much. Hand-in-hand, those silver-haired lovers would stroll the halls, visiting their friends, passing out love. They were the "romantics" of the retirement center.

When I realized that my mother's condition was worsening, I wrote her a letter of acknowledgment. I told her how much I loved her. I apologized for my orneriness when I was growing up. I told her that she was a great mother and I was proud to be her son. I told her things I had wanted to say for a long time but had been too stubborn to say until I realized she might not be in a position to comprehend the love behind the words. It was a detailed letter of love and of completion. My dad told me she often spent hours reading and re-reading that letter.

It saddened me to know that my mom no longer

knew I was her son. She would often ask, "Now, what was your name?" and I would proudly reply that my name was Larry and I was her son. She would smile and reach for my hand. I wish I could once again experience that special touch.

On one of my visits, I stopped by the local malt shop and bought my mother and father each a strawberry malt. I stopped by her room first, re-introduced myself to her, chatted for a few minutes and then took the other strawberry malt to my dad's room.

By the time I returned, she had almost finished the malt. She had lain down on the bed for a rest. She was awake. We both smiled when she saw me come into the room.

Without a word, I pulled a chair close to the bed and reached over to hold her hand. It was a divine connection. I silently affirmed my love for her. In the quiet I could feel the magic of our unconditional love, even though I knew she was quite unaware of who was holding her hand. Or was she holding my hand?

After about 10 minutes, I felt her give my hand a tender squeeze . . . three squeezes. They were brief and instantly I knew what she was saying without having to hear any words.

The miracle of unconditional love is nurtured by the power of the Divine and our own imagination.

I couldn't believe it! Even though she could no longer express her innermost thoughts like she used to, no words were necessary. It was as though she came back for a brief moment.

Many years ago when my father and she were dating, she had invented this special way of telling my dad, "I love you!" while they were sitting in church. He would softly give her hand two squeezes to say, "Me too!"

I gave her hand two soft squeezes. She turned her head and gave me a loving smile I shall never forget. Her countenance radiated love.

I remembered her expressions of unconditional love for my father, our family and her countless friends. Her love continues to profoundly influence my life.

Another eight to ten minutes went by. No words were spoken.

Suddenly, she turned to me and quietly spoke these words: "It's important to have someone who loves you."

I wept. They were tears of joy. I gave her a warm and tender hug, told her how very much I loved her and left.

My mother passed away shortly after that.

Very few words were spoken that day; those she spoke were words of gold. I will always treasure those special moments.

Larry James

The Little Glass Chip

Quite often my mother would request me to set the family table with the "good china." Because this occurred with such frequency, I never questioned these occasions. I assumed it was just my mother's desire, a momentary whim, and did what I was asked.

One evening as I was setting the table, Marge, a neighbor woman, dropped by unexpectedly. She knocked on the door and Mother, busy at the stove, called to her to come in. Marge entered the large kitchen and, glancing at the beautifully set table, remarked, "Oh, I see you're expecting company. I'll come back another time. I should have called first anyway."

"No, no, it's all right," replied my mother. "We're not expecting company."

"Well then," said Marge with a puzzled look on her face, "why would you have the good china out? I use my good china only twice a year, if that."

"Because," my mom answered laughing softly, "I've prepared my family's favorite meal. If you set your best table for special guests and outsiders when you prepare a meal, why not for your own family? They are as special as anyone I can think of."

"Well yes, but your beautiful china will get

broken," responded Marge, still not understanding the importance of the value my mother had assigned to esteeming her family in this way.

"Oh well," said Mom casually, "a few chips in the china is a small price to pay for the way we always feel as we gather as a family at the dinner table, using these lovely dishes. Besides," she added with a girlish twinkle in her eyes, "all these chips have a story to tell, now don't they?" She looked at Marge as though this woman with two grown children should have known this.

Mom walked to the cupboard and took down a plate. Holding it up she said, "See this chip? I was 17 when this happened. I'll never forget that day." My mother's voice softened and she seemed to be remembering another time. "One fall day, my brothers needed help putting the last of the season's hay up, so they hired a young, strong, handsome buck to help out. My mother had asked me to go to the hen house to gather fresh eggs. It was then that I first noticed the new help. I stopped and watched for a moment as he slung large heavy bales of fresh green hay up and over his shoulder, tossing them effortlessly into the hay mow. I tell you, he was one gorgeous man: lean, slim-waisted with powerful arms and shiny thick hair. He must have felt my presence because with a bale of hay in mid-air, he stopped, turned and looked at me, and just smiled. He was so incredibly handsome," she said slowly, running a finger around the plate, stroking it gently.

"Well, I guess my brothers took a liking to him because they invited him to have dinner with us. When my older brother directed him to sit next to me at the table, I nearly died. You can imagine how embarrassed I felt because he had seen me standing there staring at him. Now, here I was seated next to him. His presence made me so flustered, I was tongue-tied and just stared down at the table."

Suddenly remembering that she was telling a story in the presence of her young daughter and the neighbor woman, Mom blushed and hurriedly brought the story to conclusion. "Well anyway, he handed me his plate and asked that I dish him a helping. I was so nervous that my palms were sweaty and my hands shook. When I took his plate, it slipped and cracked against the casserole dish, knocking out a chip."

"Well," said Marge, unmoved by my mother's story, "I'd say that sounds like a memory I'd try to forget."

"On the contrary," countered my mother. "One year later I married that marvelous man. And to this day, when I see that plate, I fondly recall the day I met him." She carefully put the plate back into the cupboard—behind the others, in a place all its own, and seeing me staring at her, gave me a quick wink.

Aware that the passionate story she had just told held no sentiments for Marge, she hurriedly took down another plate, this time one that had been shattered and then carefully pieced back together, with small droplets of glue dribbled out of rather crooked seams. "This plate was broken the day we brought our newborn son, Mark, home from the hospital," Mom said. "What a cold and blustery day that was! Trying to be helpful, my six-year-old daughter dropped that plate as she carried it to the sink. At first I was upset, but then I told myself, "It's just a broken plate and I won't let a broken plate change the happiness we feel welcoming this new baby to our family. As I recall, we all had a lot of fun on the several attempts it took to glue *that* plate together!"

I was *sure* my mother had other stories to tell about that set of china.

Several days passed and I couldn't forget about *that*

plate. It had been made special, if for no other reason, because Mom had stored it carefully *behind* the others. There was something about that plate that intrigued me and thoughts of it lingered in the back of my mind.

A few days later my mother took a trip into town to get groceries. As usual I was put in charge of caring for the other children when she was gone. As the car drove out of the driveway, I did what I always did in the first ten minutes when she left for town. I ran into my parents' bedroom (as I was forbidden to do!), pulled up a chair, opened the top dresser drawer and snooped through the drawer, as I had done so many times before. There in the back of the drawer, beneath soft and wonderful smelling grown-up garments, was a small square wooden jewelry box. I took it out and opened it. In it were the usual items: the red ruby ring left to my mother by Auntie Hilda, her favorite aunt; a pair of delicate pearl earrings given to my mother's mom by her husband on their wedding day; and my mother's dainty wedding ring, which she often took off as she helped do outside chores alongside her husband.

Once again enchanted by these precious keepsakes, I did what every little girl would want to do: I tried them all on, filling my mind with glorious images of what I thought it must be like to be grown up, to be a beautiful woman like my mother, and to own such exquisite things. I couldn't wait to be old enough to command a drawer of my very own and be able to tell others they could *not* go into it!

Today I didn't linger too long on these thoughts. I removed the fine piece of red felt on the lid of the little wooden box that separated the jewelry from an ordinary-looking chip of white glass—heretofore, completely meaningless to me. I removed the piece of glass from the box, held it up to the light to examine it more carefully, and following an instinct, ran to the kitchen cabinet, pulled up a chair and climbed up and took down the plate. Just as I had imagined, the chip—so carefully stored beneath the only three precious keepsakes my mother owned—belonged to the plate she had broken on the day she first laid eyes on my father.

Wiser now, and with more respect, I cautiously returned the sacred chip to its place beneath the jewels along with the piece of fabric that protected it. Now I knew for sure that the china held for Mother a number of love stories about her family, but none so memorable as the legacy she had assigned to *that* plate. With that chip began a love story of love stories, now in its 53rd chapter; my parents have been married for 53 years!

One of my sisters asked my mother if someday the antique ruby ring could be hers, and my other sister has laid claim to Grandmother's pearl earrings. I want my sisters to have these beautiful family heirlooms. As for me, well, I'd like the memento representing the beginning of a very extraordinary woman's extraordinary life of loving. I'd like that little glass chip.

Bettie B. Youngs

It Takes Courage

You gain strength, experience and confidence by every experience where you really stop to look fear in the face. . . . You must do the thing you cannot do.

Eleanor Roosevelt

Her name is Nikki. She lives just down the road from me. I have been inspired by this young lady for a number of years. Her story has touched my heart and when times get tough, I reflect on her courage.

It started when she was in the seventh grade, with the doctor's report. Everything that her family had feared was true. The diagnosis: leukemia. The next few months were filled with regular visits to the hospital. She was poked and jabbed and tested hundreds and thousands of times. Then came the chemotherapy. Along with it, and a chance to possibly save her life, she lost her hair. Losing your hair as a seventh grader is a devastating thing. The hair didn't grow back. The family started to worry.

That summer before the eighth grade she bought a wig. It felt uncomfortable, it was scratchy, but she wore it. She was very popular and loved by so many students. She was a cheerleader and always had other kids around her, but things seemed to change. She looked strange, and you know how kids are. I guess maybe like the rest of us. Sometimes we go after laughter and do things even though it causes great pain in someone else. The wig was pulled off from behind about a half a dozen times in the first two weeks of the eighth grade. She would stop, bend down, shake from fear and embarrassment, put her wig back on, wipe away the tears and walk to class, always wondering why no one stood up for her.

This went on for two agonizing, hellish weeks. She told her parents she couldn't take it anymore. They said, "You can stay home if you wish." You see, if your daughter is dying in the eighth grade, you don't care if she makes it to the ninth. Having her happy and giving her a chance at peace is all that matters. Nikki told me that to lose her hair is nothing. She said, "I can handle that." She even said that losing her life is of little concern. "I can handle that, too," she said, "but do you know what it's like to lose your friends? To walk down the hall and have them part like the Red Sea because you're coming, to go into the cafeteria on pizza day, our best meal, and have them leave with half-eaten plates? They say that they're not hungry but you know that they're leaving because you're sitting there. Do you know what it's like to have no one want to sit next to you in math class and the kids in the locker to the left and right of you have pulled out? They're putting their books in with someone else, all because they might have to stand next to the girl wearing the wig, the one with the weird disease. It's not even catching. They can't get it from me. Don't they know that I need my friends most of all? Oh, yes," she said, "losing your life is nothing when you know that because of your belief in God you know exactly where you're going to spend eternity. Losing your hair is nothing either, but losing your friends is so devastating."

She had planned to stay home from school, but something happened that weekend. She heard about two boys, one in the sixth grade, one in the seventh, and their stories gave her the courage to go on. The seventh-grader was from Arkansas and even though it wasn't popular, he took his *New Testament Bible* in his shirt to school. As the story goes, three boys approached him, grabbed the Bible and said, "You sissy. Religion is for sissies. Prayer is for sissies. Don't ever again bring this Bible back to school." He reportedly handed the Bible back to the biggest one of the three and said, "Here, see if you've got enough courage to carry this around school just one day." They said that he made three friends.

The next story that inspired Nikki was a sixth-grader from Ohio named Jimmy Masterdino. He was jealous of California because California had a state motto, "Eureka!" Ohio didn't have any. He came up with six life-changing words. He single-handedly got enough signatures. With his petitions full, he took it before the State Legislature. Today, because of a brave sixth grader, the official state motto for Ohio is "All things are possible with God."

With Nikki's new-found courage and inspiration, she put her wig on that next Monday morning. She got dressed as pretty and as fancy as she could. She told her mom and dad, "I'm going back to school today. There's something I've got to do. There's something I've got to find out." They didn't know what she meant and they were worried, fearing the worst, but they drove her to school. Every day for the last several weeks, Nikki would hug and kiss her mom and dad in the car before she got out. As unpopular as this was and even though many kids sneered and jeered at her, she never let it stop her. Today was different. She hugged and kissed them, but as she got out of the car, she turned quietly and said, "Mom and Dad, guess what I'm going to do today?" Her eyes were filling up with tears, but they were tears of joy and strength. Oh, yes, there was fear of the unknown, but she had a cause. They said, "What, baby?" She said, "Today I'm going to find out who my best friend is. Today I'm going to find out who my real friends are." And with that she grabbed the wig off her head and she set it on the seat beside her. She said, "They take me for who I am, Daddy, or they don't take me at all. I don't have much time left. I've got to find out who they are today." She started to walk, took two steps, then turned and said, "Pray for me." They said, "We are, baby." And as she walked toward 600 kids, she could hear her dad say, "That's my girl."

A miracle happened that day. She walked through that playground, into that school, and not one loud-mouth or bully, no one, made fun of the little girl with all the courage.

Nikki has taught thousands of people that to be yourself, to use your own God-given talent, and to stand up for what is right even in the midst of uncertainty, pain, fear and persecution is the only true way to live.

Nikki has since graduated from high school. The marriage that was never supposed to take place happened a few years later, and Nikki is the proud mother of a little girl that she named after my little girl, Emily. Every time something that seems impossible comes before me, I think of Nikki and I gain strength.

Bill Sanders

Be Yourself

In the world to come I shall not be asked, "Why were you not Moses?" I should be asked, "Why were you not Zusya?"

Rabbi Zusya

Ever since I was a little kid, I didn't want to be me. I wanted to be like Billy Widdledon, and Billy Widdledon didn't even like me. I walked like he walked; I talked like he talked; and I signed up for the high school he signed up for.

Which was why Billy Widdledon changed. He began to hang around Herby Vandeman; he walked like Herby Vandeman; he talked like Herby Vandeman. He mixed me up! I began to walk and talk like Billy Widdledon, who was walking and talking like Herby Vandeman.

And then it dawned on me that Herby Vandeman walked and talked like Joey Haverlin. And Joey Haverlin walked and talked like Corky Sabinson.

So here I am walking and talking like Billy Widdledon's imitation of Herby Vandeman's version of Joey Haverlin, trying to walk and talk like Corky Sabinson. And who do you think Corky Sabinson is always walking and talking like? Of all people, Dopey Wellington—that little pest who walks and talks like me!

Author unknown, submitted by Scott Shuman

• • • • •

President Calvin Coolidge once invited friends from his hometown to dine at the White House. Worried about their table manners, the guests decided to do everything that Coolidge did. This strategy succeeded, until coffee was served. The president poured his coffee into the saucer. The guests did the same. Coolidge added sugar and cream. His guests did, too. Then Coolidge bent over and put his saucer on the floor for the cat.

Erik Oleson

• • • • •

You do not have to be your mother unless she is who you want to be. You do not have to be your mother's mother, or your mother's mother's mother, or even your grandmother's mother on your father's side. You may inherit their chins or their hips or their eyes, but you are not destined to become the women who came before you. You are not destined to live their lives. So if you inherit something, inherit their strength, their resilience. Because the only person you are destined to become is the person you decide to be.

Pam Finger

• • • • •

When I get that championship I'm gonna put on my old jeans and get an old hat and grow a beard and I'm gonna walk down an old country road where nobody knows me till I find a pretty little fox who don't know my name, who just loves me for who I am. And then I'll take her back to my $250,000 house overlooking my million-dollar housing development, and I'll show her all my Cadillacs and the indoor pool in case it rains, and I'll tell her, "This is yours, honey, cause you love me for who I am."

Muhammad Ali

I Don't Despair About Kids Today

Sometimes when I'm flying from one speaking engagement to another, I find myself sitting next to someone who's quite talkative. This is often a pleasant experience for me because I'm an inveterate people-watcher. I learn so much by watching and listening to the people I meet and see every day. I've heard stories of sadness and others of delight, fear and joy, and others that would rival those on "Oprah" and "Geraldo."

Sad to say, there are times when I'm sitting next to someone who just wants to vent his spleen or inflict his political views on a captive audience for 600 miles. It was one of those days. I settled in, resignedly, as my seatmate began his disquisition on the terrible state of the world with the timeworn, "You know, kids today are . . ." He went on and on, sharing vague notions of the terrible state of teens and young adults, based on watching the six o'clock news rather selectively.

When I gratefully disembarked that plane and finally made it to my hotel in Indianapolis, I bought the local paper and went to have dinner in the hotel. There, on an inside page, was an article I believe ought to have been the front-page headline news.

In a little Indiana town, there was a 15-year-old boy with a brain tumor. He was undergoing radiation and chemotherapy treatments. As a result of those treatments, he had lost all of his hair. I don't know about you, but I remember how I would have felt about that at his age—I would have been mortified!

This young man's classmates spontaneously came to the rescue: all the boys in his grade asked their mothers if they could shave their heads so that Brian wouldn't be the only bald boy in the high school. There, on that page, was a photograph of a mother shaving off all of her son's hair with the family looking on approvingly. And in the background, a group of similarly bald young men.

No, I don't despair about kids today.

Hanoch McCarty, Ed.D.

The Flower

"I have many flowers," he said, "but the children are the most beautiful flowers of all."

Oscar Wilde

For some time I have had a person provide me with a rose boutonniere to pin on the lapel of my suit every Sunday. Because I always got a flower on Sunday morning, I really did not think much of it. It was a nice gesture that I appreciated, but it became routine. One Sunday, however, what I considered ordinary became very special.

As I was leaving the Sunday service a young man approached me. He walked right up to me and said, "Sir, what are you going to do with your flower?" At first I did not know what he was talking about, but then I understood.

I said, "Do you mean this?" as I pointed to the rose pinned to my coat.

He said, "Yes sir. I would like it if you are just going to throw it away." At this point I smiled and gladly told him that he could have my flower, casually asking him what he was going to do with it. The little boy, who was probably less than 10 years old, looked up at me and said, "Sir, I'm going to give it to my granny. My mother and father got divorced last year. I was living with my mother, but when she married again, she wanted me to live with my father. I lived with him for a while, but he said I could not stay, so he sent me to live with my grandmother. She is so good to me. She cooks for me and takes care of me. She has been so good to me that I want to give that pretty flower to her for loving me."

When the little boy finished I could hardly speak. My eyes filled with tears and I knew I had been touched in the depths of my soul. I reached up and unpinned my flower. With the flower in my hand, I looked at the boy and said, "Son, that is the nicest thing I have ever heard, but you can't have this flower because it's not enough. If you'll look in front of the pulpit, you'll see a big bouquet of flowers. Different families buy them for the church each week. Please take those flowers to your granny because she deserves the very best."

If I hadn't been touched enough already, he made one last statement and I will always cherish it. He said, "What a wonderful day! I asked for one flower but got a beautiful bouquet."

Pastor John R. Ramsey

Practice Random Kindness and Senseless Acts of Beauty

It's an underground slogan that's spreading across the nation.

It's a crisp winter day in San Francisco. A woman in a red Honda, Christmas presents piled high in the back, drives up to the Bay Bridge toll booth. "I'm paying for myself, and for the six cars behind me," she says with a smile, handing over seven commuter tickets.

One after another, the next six drivers arrive at the toll booth, dollars in hand, only to be told, "Some lady up ahead already paid your fare. Have a nice day."

The woman in the Honda, it turned out, had read something on an index card taped to a friend's refrigerator: "Practice random kindness and senseless acts of beauty." The phrase seemed to leap out at her, and she copied it down.

Judy Foreman spotted the same phrase spray-painted on a warehouse wall a hundred miles from her home. When it stayed on her mind for days, she gave up and drove all the way back to copy it down. "I thought it was incredibly beautiful," she said, explaining why she's taken to writing it at the bottom of all her letters, "like a message from above."

Her husband, Frank, liked the phrase so much that

he put it up on the classroom wall for his seventh-graders, one of whom was the daughter of a local columnist. The columnist put it in the paper, admitting that though she liked it, she didn't know where it came from or what it really meant.

Two days later, she heard from Anne Herbert. Tall, blonde and forty, Herbert lives in Marin, one of the country's ten richest counties, where she house-sits, takes odd jobs, gets by. It was in a Sausalito restaurant that Herbert jotted the phrase down on a paper placemat, after turning it around in her mind for days.

"That's wonderful!" a man sitting nearby said, and copied it down carefully on his own placemat.

"Here's the idea," Herbert says. "Anything you think there should be more of, do it randomly."

Her own fantasies include: (1) breaking into depressing-looking schools to paint the classrooms, (2) leaving hot meals on kitchen tables in the poor part of town, (3) slipping money into a proud old woman's purse. Says Herbert, "Kindness can build on itself as much as violence can."

Now the phrase is spreading, on bumper stickers, on walls, at the bottom of letters and business cards. And as it spreads, so does a vision of guerrilla goodness.

In Portland, Oregon, a man might plunk a coin into a stranger's parking meter just in time. In Paterson, New Jersey, a dozen people with pails and mops and tulip bulbs might descend on a run-down house and clean it from top to bottom while the frail elderly owners look on, dazed and smiling. In Chicago, a teenage boy may be shoveling off a driveway when the impulse strikes. What the hell, nobody's looking, he thinks, and shovels the neighbor's driveway too.

It's positive anarchy, disorder, a sweet disturbance. A woman in Boston writes "Merry Christmas!" to the tellers on the back of her checks. A man in St. Louis, whose car has just been rear-ended by a young woman, waves her away, saying, "It's a scratch. Don't worry."

Senseless acts of beauty spread: A man plants daffodils along the roadway, his shirt billowing in the breeze from passing cars. In Seattle, a man appoints himself a one-man vigilante sanitation service and roams the concrete hills collecting litter in a supermarket cart. In Atlanta, a man scrubs graffiti from a green park bench.

They say you can't smile without cheering yourself up a little—likewise, you can't commit a random kindness without feeling as if your own troubles have been lightened if only because the world has become a slightly better place.

And you can't be a recipient without feeling a shock, a pleasant jolt. If you were one of those rush-hour drivers who found your bridge fare paid, who knows what you might have been inspired to do for someone else later? Wave someone on in the intersection? Smile at a tired clerk? Or something larger, greater? Like all revolutions, guerrilla goodness begins slowly, with a single act. Let it be yours.

Adair Lara

Two Brothers

Two brothers worked together on the family farm. One was married and had a large family. The other was single. At the day's end, the brothers shared everything equally, produce and profit.

Then one day the single brother said to himself, "It's not right that we should share equally the produce and the profit. I'm alone and my needs are simple." So each night he took a sack of grain from his bin and crept across the field between their houses, dumping it into his brother's bin.

Meanwhile, the married brother said to himself, "It's not right that we should share the produce and the profit equally. After all, I'm married and I have my wife and children to look after me in years to come. My brother has no one, and no one to take care of his future." So each night he took a sack of grain and dumped it into his single brother's bin.

Both men were puzzled for years because their supply of grain never dwindled. Then one dark night the two brothers bumped into each other. Slowly it dawned on them what was happening. They dropped their sacks and embraced one another.

Author Unknown
from More Sower's Seeds *by Brian Cavanaugh*

The Heart

The best and most beautiful things in the world cannot be seen, nor touched . . . but are felt in the heart.

Helen Keller

My wife and I separated in late December and, as you might expect, I had a very difficult January. During a therapy session to help me handle the emotional turmoil stirred up by the split, I asked my therapist to give me something to help me in my new life. I had no idea whether she would agree and, if she did, I had no idea what she might offer.

I was happy that she immediately did agree and, as I expected, she gave me something totally unexpected! She handed me a heart, a small handmade Play-Doh® heart, brightly and lovingly painted. It had been given to her by a previous male client who had also gone through a divorce and who, like myself, had difficulty accessing his feelings. She added that it was not for me to keep, but only to hold onto until I got my own heart. Then I must return it to her. I understood that she was giving me a physical heart as a visual goal or as some kind of material representation of my own quest for a richer emotional life. I accepted it with anticipation of deeper emotional connections to come.

Little did I realize how quickly that wonderful gift would actually start to work.

After the session, I placed the heart carefully on the dash of my car and drove excitedly to pick up my daughter Juli-Ann, for this was the first night that she would be sleeping over at my new home. As she got into the car, she was immediately drawn to the heart, picking it up, examining it and asking me what it was. I was unsure whether I should explain the full psychological background because, after all, she was still a child. But I decided that I would tell her.

"It's a present from my therapist to help me through this difficult time and it is not for me to keep, but only to have till I get my own heart," I explained. Juli-Ann made no comment. I wondered again if I should have told her. At 11 years old, could she understand? What possible idea could she have of the huge chasm I was attempting to bridge to break my old patterns and develop deeper, richer loving connections with people?

Weeks later, when my daughter was again at my home, she handed me my Valentine's Day present early: a small box that she had painted red, tied daintily with a gold band, topped by a chocolate that we shared. With anticipation, I reached into the pretty little box. To my surprise, I pulled out a Play-Doh® heart that she had made for me and painted. I looked quizzically at her, wondering what it meant. Why was she giving me a replica of what my therapist had given me?

Then she slowly handed me a card she had made. She was embarrassed about the card but then finally allowed me to open it and read it. It was a poem far beyond her years. She had understood totally the meaning of the gift from my therapist. Juli-Ann had written me the most touching and loving poem I have ever read. Tears flooded my eyes and my heart burst open:

For My Dad

Here is a heart
For you to keep
For the big leap
You're trying to take.

Have fun on your journey.
It might be blurry.

But when you get there,
Learn to care.

Happy Valentine's Day
Love, Your Daughter, Juli-Ann

Above all my material wealth, I count this poem as my most sacred treasure.

Raymond L. Aaron

Do It Now!

*If we discovered that we had only five min-
utes left to say all that we wanted to say,
every telephone booth would be occupied by
people calling other people to stammer that
they loved them.*

Christopher Morley

In a class I teach for adults, I recently did the "unpar-
donable." I gave the class homework! The assignment
was to "go to someone you love within the next week
and tell them you love them. It has to be someone you
have never said those words to before or at least
haven't shared those words with for a long time."

Now that doesn't sound like a very tough assignment, until you stop to realize that most of the men in
that group were over 35 and were raised in the generation of men that were taught that expressing emotions is not "macho." Showing feelings or crying
(heaven forbid!) was just not done. So this was a very
threatening assignment for some.

At the beginning of our next class, I asked if someone wanted to share what happened when they told
someone they loved them. I fully expected one of the
women to volunteer, as was usually the case, but on

this evening one of the men raised his hand. He appeared quite moved and a bit shaken.

As he unfolded out of his chair (all 6'2" of him), he began by saying, "Dennis, I was quite angry with you last week when you gave us this assignment. I didn't feel that I had anyone to say those words to, and besides, who were you to tell me to do something that personal? But as I began driving home my conscience started talking to me. It was telling me that I knew exactly who I needed to say 'I love you' to. You see, five years ago, my father and I had a vicious disagreement and really never resolved it since that time. We avoided seeing each other unless we absolutely had to at Christmas or other family gatherings. But even then, we hardly spoke to each other. So, last Tuesday by the time I got home I had convinced myself I was going to tell my father I loved him.

"It's weird, but just making that decision seemed to lift a heavy load off my chest.

"When I got home, I rushed into the house to tell my wife what I was going to do. She was already in bed, but I woke her up anyway. When I told her, she didn't just get out of bed, she catapulted out and hugged me, and for the first time in our married life she saw me cry. We stayed up half the night drinking coffee and talking. It was great!

"The next morning I was up bright and early. I was so excited I could hardly sleep. I got to the office early and accomplished more in two hours than I had the whole day before.

"At 9:00 I called my dad to see if I could come over after work. When he answered the phone, I just said, 'Dad, can I come over after work tonight? I have something to tell you.' My dad responded with a grumpy, 'Now what?' I assured him it wouldn't take long, so he finally agreed.

"At 5:30, I was at my parents' house ringing the doorbell, praying that Dad would answer the door. I was afraid if Mom answered that I would chicken out and tell her instead. But as luck would have it, Dad did answer the door.

"I didn't waste any time—I took one step in the door and said, 'Dad, I just came over to tell you that I love you.'

"It was as if a transformation came over my dad. Before my eyes his face softened, the wrinkles seemed to disappear and he began to cry. He reached out and hugged me and said, 'I love you too, son, but I've never been able to say it.'

"It was such a precious moment I didn't want to move. Mom walked by with tears in her eyes. I just waved and blew her a kiss. Dad and I hugged for a moment longer and then I left. I hadn't felt that great in a long time.

"But that's not even my point. Two days after that visit, my dad, who had heart problems but didn't tell me, had an attack and ended up in the hospital, unconscious. I don't know if he'll make it.

"So my message to all of you in this class is this: Don't wait to do the things you know need to be done. What if I had waited to tell my dad—maybe I will never get the chance again! Take the time to do what you need to do and *do it now!*"

Dennis E. Mannering

CALVIN AND HOBBES By Bill Watterson

CALVIN AND HOBBES© Watterson. Reprinted with permission of Universal Press Syndicate.
All rights reserved.

The Martyrdom of Andy

Andy was a sweet, amusing little guy whom every-one liked but harassed, just because that was the way one treated Andy Drake. He took the kidding well. He always smiled back with those great big eyes that seemed to say, "Thank you, thank you, thank you," with each sweeping blink.

For us fifth-graders, Andy was our outlet; he was our whipping boy. He even seemed grateful to pay this special price for membership in our group.

> *Andy Drake don't eat no cake,*
> *And his sister don't eat no pie.*
> *If it wasn't for the welfare dole,*
> *All the Drakes would die.*

Andy even appeared to like this sing-song parody of Jack Spratt. The rest of us really enjoyed it, bad grammar and all.

I don't know why Andy had to endure this special treatment to deserve our friendship and membership in the group. It just evolved naturally—no vote or discussion.

I don't recall that it was ever mentioned that Andy's father was in prison or that his mother took in washing and men. Or that Andy's ankles, elbows and fingernails were always dirty and his old coat was way too big. We soon wore all the fun out of that. Andy never fought back.

Snobbery blossoms in the very young, I guess. It's clear now the group attitude was that it was our right to belong to the group but that Andy was a member by our sufferance.

Despite that, we all liked Andy until that day— until that very moment.

"He's different!" "We don't want him, do we?"

Which one of us said it? I've wanted to blame Randolph all these years, but I can't honestly say who spoke those trigger words that brought out the savagery lying dormant but so near the surface in all of us. It doesn't matter who, for the fervor with which we took up the cry revealed us all.

"I didn't want to do what we did."

For years I tried to console myself with that. Then one day, I stumbled on those unwelcome but irrefutable words that convicted me forever:

> *The hottest corners of hell are reserved for those who, during a moment of crisis, maintain their neutrality.*

The weekend was to be like others the group had enjoyed together. After school on a Friday we would meet at the home of one of the members—mine this time—for a camp-out in the nearby woods. Our mothers, who did most of the preparation for these "safaris," fixed an extra pack for Andy who was to join us after chores.

We quickly made camp, mothers' apron strings forgotten. With individual courage amplified by the group, we were now "men" against the jungle.

The others told me that since it was my party, I should be the one to give Andy the news!

Me? I who had long believed that Andy secretly thought a little more of me than he did the others because of the puppy-like way he looked at me? I who often felt him revealing his love and appreciation with those huge, wide-open eyes?

I can still plainly see Andy as he came toward me down the long, dark tunnel of trees that leaked only enough of the late afternoon light to kaleidoscope changing patterns on his soiled old sweatshirt. Andy was on his rusty, one-of-a-kind bike—a girl's model with sections of garden hose wired to the rims for tires. He appeared excited and happier than I had ever seen him, this frail little guy who had been an adult all his life. I knew he was savoring the acceptance by the group, this first chance to belong, to have "boy fun," to do "boy things."

Andy waved to me as I stood in the camp clearing awaiting him. I ignored his happy greeting. He vaulted off the funny old bike and trotted over toward me, full of joy and conversation. The others, concealed within the tent, were quiet but I felt their support.

Why won't he get serious? Can't he see that I am not returning his gaiety? Can't he see by now that his babblings aren't reaching me?

Then suddenly he did see! His innocent countenance opened even more, leaving him totally vulnerable. His whole demeanor said, "It's going to be very bad, isn't it, Ben? Let's have it." Undoubtedly well-practiced in facing disappointment, he didn't even brace for the blow. Andy never fought back.

Incredulously, I heard myself say, "Andy, we don't want you."

Hauntingly vivid still is the stunning quickness with which two huge tears sprang into Andy's eyes and just stayed there. Vivid because of a million maddening reruns of that scene in my mind. The way Andy looked at me—frozen for an eternal moment—

what was it? It wasn't hate. Was it shock? Was it disbelief? Or, was it pity—for me?

Or forgiveness?

Finally, a fleet little tremor broke across Andy's lips and he turned without appeal, or even a question, to make the long, lonely trip home in the dark.

As I entered the tent, someone—the last one of us to feel the full weight of the moment—started the old doggerel:

> Andy Drake don't eat no cake,
> And his sister don't . . .

Then it was unanimous! No vote taken, no word spoken, but we all knew. We knew that we had done something horribly, cruelly wrong. We were swept over by the delayed impact of dozens of lessons and sermons. We heard for the first time, "Inasmuch as ye do it unto the least of these . . ."

In that hushed, heavy moment, we gained an understanding new to us but indelibly fixed in our minds: We had destroyed an individual made in the image of God with the only weapon for which he had no defense and we had no excuse—rejection.

Andy's poor attendance in school made it difficult to tell when he actually withdrew, but one day it dawned on me that he was gone forever. I had spent too many days struggling within myself to find and polish a proper way of telling Andy how totally, consummately ashamed and sorry I was, and am. I now know that to have hugged Andy and to have cried with him and even to have joined with him in a long silence would have been enough. It may have healed us both.

I never saw Andy Drake again. I have no idea where he went or where he is, if he is.

But to say I haven't seen Andy is not entirely accurate. In the decades since that autumn day in the

Arkansas woods, I have encountered thousands of Andy Drakes. My conscience places Andy's mask over the face of every disadvantaged person with whom I come in contact. Each one stares back at me with that same haunting, expectant look that became fixed in my mind that day long ago.

> *Dear Andy Drake:*
>
> *The chance you will ever see these words is quite remote, but I must try. It's much too late for this confession to purge my conscience of guilt. I neither expect it to nor want it to.*
>
> *What I do pray for, my little friend of long ago, is that you might somehow learn of and be lifted by the continuing force of your sacrifice. What you suffered at my hands that day and the loving courage you showed, God has twisted, turned and molded into a blessing. This knowledge might ease the memory of that terrible day for you.*
>
> *I've been no saint, Andy, nor have I done all the things I could and should have done with my life. But what I want you to know is that I have never again knowingly betrayed an Andy Drake. Nor, I pray, shall I ever.*
>
> *Ben Burton*

Heaven and Hell—
The Real Difference

A man spoke with the Lord about heaven and hell. The Lord said to the man, "Come, I will show you hell." They entered a room where a group of people sat around a huge pot of stew. Everyone was famished, desperate and starving. Each held a spoon that reached the pot, but each spoon had a handle so much longer than their own arm that it could not be used to get the stew into their own mouths. The suffering was terrible.

"Come, now I will show you heaven," the Lord said after a while. They entered another room, identical to the first—the pot of stew, the group of people, the same long-handled spoons. But there everyone was happy and well-nourished.

"I don't understand," said the man. "Why are they happy here when they were miserable in the other room and everything was the same?"

The Lord smiled. "Ah, it is simple," he said. "Here they have learned to feed each other."

Ann Landers

Grandmother's Gift

For as long as I can remember, I have called my grandmother Gagi. "Gaga" was the first word that came out of my mouth as a baby, and my proud grandmother was sure that I was trying to say her name. She has remained my Gagi to this day.

At the time of my grandfather's death, at 90 years of age, my grandparents had been married for over 50 years. Gagi felt the loss deeply. The central focus had been taken from her life, and she retreated from the world, entering into an extended period of mourning. Her grieving lasted nearly five years, and during that time I made it a conscious habit to visit her every week or two.

One day I went to visit Gagi expecting to find her in her usual state of quiescence that I had come to know so well since my grandfather's passing. Instead, I found her sitting in her wheelchair beaming. When I didn't comment quickly enough about the obvious change in her demeanor, she confronted me.

"Don't you want to know why I'm so happy? Aren't you even curious?"

"Of course, Gagi," I apologized. "Forgive me for not responding quickly enough. Tell me, why are you so happy? Why this new disposition?"

"Because last night I got an answer," she declared. "I finally know why God took your grandfather and left me behind to live without him."

Gagi was always full of surprises, but I have to admit that I was really taken aback by this statement. "Why, Gagi?" I managed.

Then, as if imparting the greatest secret in the world, she lowered her voice, leaned forward in her wheelchair and confided quietly, "Your grandfather knew that the secret of life is love, and he lived it every day. He had become unconditional love in action. I have known about unconditional love, but I haven't fully lived it. That's why he got to go first, and I had to stay behind."

She paused as if considering what she was about to say, and then continued, "All this time I thought I was being punished for something, but last night I found out that I was left behind as a gift from God. He let me stay so that I too could turn my life into love. You see," she continued, pointing a finger to the sky, "last night I was shown that you can't learn the lesson out there. Love has to be lived here on earth. Once you leave, it's too late. So I was given the gift of life so that I can learn to live love here and now."

From that day, every visit became a new adventure as Gagi shared her stories regarding her goal. Once when I went to see her she pounded the arm of her wheelchair in excitement and said, "You'll never guess what I did this morning!"

When I responded that I couldn't guess, she continued excitedly, "Well, this morning your uncle was upset and angry with me over something I had done. I didn't even flinch! I received his anger, wrapped it in love and returned it with joy." Her eyes twinkled as she added, "It was even kind of fun and his anger dissolved."

Though age continued on its relentless course, her life was vigorously renewed. Visit after visit added up to the passing of years, while Gagi practiced her lessons in love. She had a purpose worth living for, a reason for going on those last 12 years.

In the last days of Gagi's life I visited her often in the hospital. As I walked toward her room one day, the nurse on duty looked into my eyes and said, "Your grandmother is a very special lady, you know . . . she's a light."

Yes, purpose lit up her life and she became a light for others until the end.

D. Trinidad Hunt

Angels Don't Need Legs to Fly

There is a land of the living and a land of the dead and the bridge is love . . .

Thornton Wilder

On one of my recent trips to Warsaw, Poland, the tour guide for our group of 30 citizen diplomats from The Human Awareness Institute in San Mateo, California, was shocked when I said we wanted to visit with people. "No more cathedrals and museums," I said, "We want to meet with people!"

The guide, whose name was Robert, said, "You are pulling my leg. You must not be Americans. Canadians, maybe. Not Americans. Americans don't want to visit with people. We watch *Dynasty* and other American TV shows. Americans are not interested in people. So tell me the truth. You are Canadians or maybe English, yes?"

Sad to say, he was not kidding. He was very serious. However, so were we! After a long discussion about "Dynasty" and other TV shows and movies, and admitting that yes, there are many Americans like that but many more who are not, we were able to convince Robert to take us to visit with people.

Robert took us to a convalescent hospital for elderly

women. The oldest woman there was over 100 years old, and she was reportedly a former Russian princess. She recited poetry to us in many languages. Although she was not very coherent at times, her grace, charm and beauty shone through and she didn't want us to leave. But we had to. Accompanied by nurses, doctors, attendants and the hospital administrator, we got to hug, laugh with and hold almost all of the 85 women in that hospital. Some called me "Poppa" and wanted me to hold them. I did, and I cried voluminously as I saw the beauty of their souls in their withered bodies.

However, the major shock of our tour was the last patient we were to visit. She was the youngest woman in the hospital. Olga was 58 years old. For the past eight years, she had sat alone in her room refusing to get out of bed. Because her beloved husband had died, she no longer wanted to live. This woman, who once was a medical doctor, had attempted suicide eight years earlier by throwing herself under a train. The train had cut off both her legs.

As I looked at this decimated woman, who had gone through the gates of hell because of her losses, I was overcome with such grief and compassion that I fell to my knees and started stroking and kissing the stumps of her legs. It was as if I were being compelled by a power much greater than myself. As I was kissing and stroking her, I was speaking to her in English. I only found out later that she did, indeed, understand me. But that was irrelevant because I hardly remembered what I said. It was something about feeling her pain and her loss, and encouraging her to use her experience to help her patients in the future with a greater compassion and empathy than ever before. And that in this time of great transition, her country needed her now more than ever. Just as her country was ravaged and decimated and was now coming back to life, so must she.

I told her that she reminded me of a wounded angel and that the Greek word angel, *angelos*, means, "messenger of love, servant of God." I also reminded her that angels don't need legs to fly. After about 15 minutes or so, everyone in the room started sobbing. As I looked up, Olga was glowing as she called for a wheelchair and started to get out of bed for the first time in eight years.

Stan Dale

He's My Dad

The following letter was dropped off at an outpatient clinic of a large teaching hospital. Although the writer's identity is unknown, its content is relevant to all those in health care.

To Each Staff Member of this Facility:

As you pick up that chart today and scan that green Medicaid card, I hope you will remember what I am about to say.

I spent yesterday with you. I was there with my mother and father. We didn't know where we were supposed to go or what we were supposed to do, for we had never needed your services before. We have never before been labeled *charity*.

I watched yesterday as my dad became a diagnosis, a chart, a case number, a charity case labeled "no sponsor" because he has no health insurance.

I saw a weak man stand in line, waiting for five hours to be shuffled through a system of impatient office workers, a burned-out nursing staff and a budget-scarce facility, being robbed of any dignity and pride he may have had left. I was amazed at how impersonal your staff was, huffing and blowing when the patient did not present the correct form, speaking carelessly of other patients' cases in front of passersby, of lunch breaks that would be spent away from this "poor man's hell."

My dad is only a green card, a file number to clutter

your desk on appointment day, a patient who will ask for directions twice after they've been mechanically given the first time. But, no, that's not really my dad. That's only what you see.

What you don't see is a cabinetmaker since the age of 14, a self-employed man who has a wonderful wife, four grown kids (who visit too much), and five grand-children (with two more on the way)—all of whom think their "pop" is the greatest. This man is every-thing a daddy should be—strong and firm, yet tender; rough around the edges, a country boy, yet respected by prominent business owners.

He's my dad, the man who raised me through thick and thin, gave me away as a bride, held my children at their births, stuffed a $20 bill into my hand when times were tough and comforted me when I cried. Now we are told that before long cancer will take this man away from us.

You may say these are the words of a grieving daughter lashing out in helplessness at the prospect of losing a loved one. I would not disagree. Yet I would urge you not to discount what I say. Never lose sight of the people behind your charts. Each chart represents a person—with feelings, a history, a life—whom you have the power to touch for one day by your words and actions. Tomorrow it may be your loved one—your relative or neighbor—who turns into a case number, a green card, a name to be marked off with a yellow marker as done for the day.

I pray that you will reward the next person you greet at your station with a kind word or smile because that person is someone's dad, husband, wife, mother, son, or daughter—or simply because he or she is a human being, created and loved by God, just as you are.

Author Unknown
Submitted by Holly Cresswell

What Goes Around
Comes Around

When I was working as a disc jockey in Columbus, Ohio, I used to go to University Hospital or Grant Hospital on my way home. I would walk down the corridors and just walk into different people's rooms and read Scripture to them or talk to them. It was a way of forgetting about my problems and being thankful to God for my health. It made a difference in the lives of those I visited. One time it literally saved my life.

I was very controversial in radio. I had offended someone in an editorial that I had done about a promoter who was bringing entertainers into town who were not the original members of a particular group. The person I exposed literally took a contract out on me!

One night I was coming home at about two o'clock in the morning. I had just finished working at a night club where I was the emcee. As I began to open my door, a man came out from behind the side of my house and said, "Are you Les Brown?"

I said, "Yes, sir."

He said, "I need to talk to you. I was sent here to carry out a contract on you."

"Me? Why?" I asked.

He said, "Well, there's a promoter that's very upset about the money you cost him when you said that the group that was coming to town was not the real group."

"Are you going to do something to me?" I asked.

He said, "No." And I didn't want to ask him why because I didn't want him to change his mind! I was just glad!

He continued, "My mother was in Grant Hospital and she wrote me about how you came in one day and sat down and talked to her and read Scripture to her. She was so impressed that this morning disc jockey, who didn't know her, came in and did that. She wrote me about you when I was in the Ohio penitentiary. I was impressed with that and I've always wanted to meet you. When I heard the word out on the street that somebody wanted to knock you off," he said, "I accepted the contract and then told them to leave you alone."

Les Brown

The Two-Dollar Bill

Returning from a trip to Washington, D.C., I arrived in Anchorage at about 2:00 A.M. on a Monday morning in the middle of May. At 9:00 A.M., I was scheduled to talk at a local high school to students in a program designed to keep pregnant teens and troubled kids in school.

The school is highly secured because most of the kids are troublemakers who become involved with the law. I found it very difficult to address this multicultural group and talk about things that could motivate them for the future. I wasn't making any headway until I started talking about what I do so well, helping people with money.

I took out a stack of $2 bills and I started giving them out. People started coming up and taking them. The kids started to wake up because it was free money. The only thing I asked them after they took the money was not to spend it on *themselves*. I told them that they each had children that are unborn and, maybe, if there is anything in this world that could help move them forward, it is the fact that someone cares enough to do this.

Some of the kids asked for my autograph, some did not. I think I honestly touched some of them. I started exchanging the dollar bills for a copy of the book I had written. This went on for five or six minutes and I finally closed with telling them about my grandfather, who had motivated me to go forward. I told them that no matter what happens, to remember that whether it is a teacher or themselves, someone out there really cares about them and is pulling for their success.

This is not the end of the story. When I left the classroom, I told them to call me if they ever had problems or if they were ever in trouble. I couldn't promise that I could help, but I was willing to listen and willing to try to do anything in the world. I also told them if they wanted a copy of my book to call my office. I would be happy to send one to them.

Three days later, I received a crumpled piece of paper in the mail. It was from a girl who heard my talk.

Dear Floyd,

Thank you very much for taking time to come and talk to my class. Thank you for giving me the crisp, new $2 bill. I will cherish this forever and I have written my child's name on it and it will never be used for anything else, but something that she wants or she needs. The reason I am writing you is because the day that you talked to our class, I had made a decision that morning. I had cleaned out my desk, paid whatever bills I owed the school, and I was going to take mine and my unborn child's life because I really didn't think anyone cared. When you told the story, it brought tears to my eyes, about someone pulling for you, that life was not ready to be terminated. The fact is I will probably stick around awhile, because there are people like you that care about people like me, that don't even know me. Thanks for caring.

Floyd L. Shilanski

The Ultimate Sacrifice

Linda Birtish literally gave herself away. Linda was an outstanding teacher who felt that if she had the time, she would like to create great art and poetry. When she was 28, however, she began to get severe headaches. Her doctors discovered that she had an enormous brain tumor. They told her that her chances of surviving an operation were about 2 percent. Therefore, rather than operate immediately, they chose to wait for six months.

She knew she had great artistry in her. So during those six months she wrote and drew feverishly. All of her poetry, except one piece, was published in magazines. All of her art, except one piece, was shown and sold at some of the leading galleries.

At the end of six months, she had the operation. The night before the operation, she decided to literally give herself away. In case of her death, she wrote a "will," in which she donated all of her body parts to those who needed them more than she would.

Unfortunately, Linda's operation was fatal. Subsequently, her eyes went to an eye bank in Bethesda, Maryland, and from there to a recipient in South Carolina. A young man, age 28, went from darkness to sight. That young man was so profoundly grateful that he wrote to the eye bank thanking them for existing. It was only the second "thank you" that the eye bank had received after giving out in excess of 30,000 eyes!

Furthermore, he said he wanted to thank the parents of the donor. They must indeed be magnificent folks to have a child who would give away her eyes. He was given the name of the Birtish family and he decided to fly in to see them on Staten Island. He arrived unannounced and rang the doorbell. After hearing his introduction, Mrs. Birtish reached out and embraced him. She said, "Young man, if you've got nowhere to go, my husband and I would love for you to spend your weekend with us."

He stayed, and as he was looking around Linda's room, he saw that she'd read Plato. He'd read Plato in Braille. She'd read Hegel. He'd read Hegel in Braille.

The next morning Mrs. Birtish was looking at him and said, "You know, I'm sure I've seen you somewhere before, but I don't know where." All of a sudden she remembered. She ran upstairs and pulled out the last picture Linda had ever drawn. It was a portrait of her ideal man.

The picture was virtually identical to this young man who had received Linda's eyes.

Then her mother read the last poem Linda had written on her deathbed. It read:

Two hearts passing in the night
falling in love
never able to gain each other's sight.

Jack Canfield and Mark Victor Hansen

2

ON PARENTING

*Children will not remember
you for the material things
you provided but for the
feeling that you cherished them.*

Richard L. Evans

ZIGGY© ZIGGY AND FRIENDS, INC. Reprinted with permission of Universal Press Syndicate.
All rights reserved.

I Owe You

When most people look through their wallets or their pocketbooks, way down at the bottom, past the credit cards, baby pictures and Green Stamps, they usually find a little ol' dog-eared piece of poetry.

I was cleaning out my wallet the other day and I ran across a whole bunch of IOUs instead, some of them 30 years overdue.

Funny thing is that all these IOUs are owed to one person and I kind of feel like right now might be a pretty good time for an accounting.

MOM, ARE YOU LISTENING?

Mom, I owe you for so many things—a lot of services. Like the night watchman, for instance—for lying awake nights listening for coughs, cries, creaking floorboards and me coming in too late. You had the eye of an eagle and the roar of a lion, but you always had a heart as big as a house.

I owe you for services as a short-order cook, chef, baker—for making sirloin out of hamburger, turkey out of tuna fish and two big ol' strapping boys out of leftovers.

I owe you for cleaning services, for the daily scrubbing of the face and ears—all work done by hand—and for the frequent dusting of a small boy's pants to try to make sure he led a spotless life. And for drying the tears of childhood and ironing out the problems of growing up, something no laundry could ever do.

I owe you for services as a bodyguard—for protecting me from the terrors of thunderstorms and nightmares and too many green apples.

And Lord knows I owe you for medical attention—for nursing me through measles, mumps, bruises, bumps, splinters and spring fever. And let's not forget medical advice either—oh, no—important things like don't scratch it or it won't get well and if you cross your eyes, they are going to stick like that. Probably the most important of all was, be sure you've got on clean underwear, boy, in case you're in an accident.

I owe you for veterinary services for feeding every lost dog I dragged home at the end of a rope and for healing the pains of puppy love.

I owe you for entertainment—entertainment that kept the household going during some pretty tough times—for wonderful productions at Christmas, Fourth of July and birthdays—and for making make-believe come true on a very limited budget.

I owe you for construction work—for building kites, confidence, hopes and dreams. Somehow you made them all touch the sky. And I owe you for cementing a family together so it could stand the worst kind of shocks and blows, and for laying down a strong foundation to build a life on.

I owe you for carrying charges—for carrying me on your books for the necessities of life that a growing boy just had to have—things like a pair of high-top boots with a little pocket on the side for a jackknife. And one thing, Mom, I will never ever forget—when there were only two pieces of apple pie left and three hungry people, you were the only one who suddenly decided you really didn't like apple pie after all.

These are just a very few of the things for which

payment is long overdue. The person I owe them to worked very cheap. She managed by simply doing without a whole lot of things that she needed for herself.

My IOUs add up to much more than I could ever hope to repay. But you know the nicest thing about it all is that I know she'd mark the entire bill "paid in full" for just one kiss and four little words—

MOM, I LOVE YOU.

Author Unknown

If I Had My Child to Raise Over Again

If I had my child to raise all over again,
I'd finger-paint more and point the finger less.
I'd do less correcting and more connecting.
I'd take my eyes off my watch, and watch with my
    eyes.
I would care to know less and know to care more.
I'd take more hikes and fly more kites.
I'd stop playing serious, and seriously play.
I'd run through more fields and gaze at more stars.
I'd do more hugging and less tugging.
I would be firm less often, and affirm much more.
I'd build self-esteem first, and the house later.
I'd teach less about the love of power,
    and more about the power of love.

Diane Loomans

From the book, *Full Esteem Ahead, 100 Ways to Build Self-Esteem* in Children & Adults. ©1994 Diane Loomans.

CALVIN AND HOBBES© Watterson. Reprinted with permission of Universal Press Syndicate.
All rights reserved.

Remember, We're Raising Children, Not Flowers!

David, my next-door neighbor, has two young kids ages five and seven. One day he was teaching his seven-year-old son Kelly how to push the gas-powered lawn mower around the yard. As he was teaching him how to turn the mower around at the end of the lawn, his wife, Jan, called to him to ask a question. As David turned to answer the question, Kelly pushed the lawn mower right through the flower bed at the edge of the lawn—leaving a two-foot wide path leveled to the ground!

When David turned back around and saw what had happened, he began to lose control. David had put a lot of time and effort into making those flower beds the envy of the neighborhood. As he began to raise his voice to his son, Jan walked quickly over to him, put her hand on his shoulder and said, "David, please remember . . . we're raising children, not flowers!"

Jan reminded me how important it is as a parent to remember our priorities. Kids and their self-esteem are more important than any physical object they might break or destroy. The window pane shattered by a baseball, a lamp knocked over by a careless child, or a plate dropped in the kitchen are already broken. The flowers are already dead. I must remember not to add to the destruction by breaking a child's spirit and deadening his sense of liveliness.

• • • • • • • • •

I was buying a sport coat a few weeks ago and Mark Michaels, the owner of the store, and I were discussing parenting. He told me that while he and his wife and seven-year-old daughter were out for dinner, his daughter knocked over her water glass. After the water was cleaned up without any recriminating remarks from her parents, she looked up and said, "You know, I really want to thank you guys for not being like other parents. Most of my friends' parents would have yelled at them and given them a lecture about paying more attention. Thanks for not doing that!"

Once, when I was having dinner with some friends, a similar incident happened. Their five-year-old son knocked over a glass of milk at the dinner table. When they immediately started in on him, I intentionally knocked my glass over, too. When I started to explain how I still knock things over even at the age of 48, the boy started to beam and the parents seemingly got the message and backed off. How easy it is to forget that we are all still learning.

• • • • • • • • •

I recently heard a story from Stephen Glenn about a famous research scientist who had made several very important medical breakthroughs. He was being interviewed by a newspaper reporter who asked him why he thought he was able to be so much more creative than the average person. What set him so far apart from others?

He responded that, in his opinion, it all came from an experience with his mother that occurred when he was about two years old. He had been trying to remove a bottle of milk from the refrigerator when he lost his grip on the slippery bottle and it fell, spilling its contents all over the kitchen floor—a veritable sea of milk!

When his mother came into the kitchen, instead of yelling at him, giving him a lecture or punishing him, she said, "Robert, what a great and wonderful mess you have made! I have rarely seen such a huge puddle of milk. Well, the damage has already been done. Would you like to get down and play in the milk for a few minutes before we clean it up?"

Indeed, he did. After a few minutes, his mother said, "You know, Robert, whenever you make a mess like this, eventually you have to clean it up and restore everything to its proper order. So, how would you like to do that? We could use a sponge, a towel or a mop. Which do you prefer?" He chose the sponge and together they cleaned up the spilled milk.

His mother then said, "You know, what we have here is a failed experiment in how to effectively carry a big milk bottle with two tiny hands. Let's go out in the back yard and fill the bottle with water and see if you can discover a way to carry it without dropping it." The little boy learned that if he grasped the bottle at the top near the lip with both hands, he could carry it without dropping it. What a wonderful lesson!

This renowned scientist then remarked that it was at that moment that he knew he didn't need to be afraid to make mistakes. Instead, he learned that mistakes were just opportunities for learning something new, which is, after all, what scientific experiments are all about. Even if the experiment "doesn't work," we usually learn something valuable from it.

Wouldn't it be great if all parents would respond the way Robert's mother responded to him?

• • • • • • • • • •

One last story that illustrates the application of this attitude in an adult context was told by Paul Harvey on the radio several years back. A young woman was driving home from work when she snagged her fender on the bumper of another car. She was in tears as she explained that it was a new car, only a few days from the showroom. How was she ever going to explain the damaged car to her husband?

The driver of the other car was sympathetic, but explained that they must note each other's license numbers and registration numbers. As the young woman reached into a large brown envelope to retrieve the documents, a piece of paper fell out. In a heavy masculine scrawl were these words: "In case of accident . . . remember, honey, it's you I love, not the car!"

• • • • • • • • • •

Let's remember that our children's spirits are more important than any material things. When we do, self-esteem and love blossom and grow more beautifully than any bed of flowers ever could.

Jack Canfield

DENNIS THE MENACE By Ketcham

*"If you're raisin' me right,
HOW COME I GET INTO SO MUCH TROUBLE?"*

DENNIS THE MENACE® used by permission of Hank Ketcham and
© by North America Syndicate.

He Is Just a Little Boy

He stands at the plate
with his heart pounding fast.
The bases are loaded,
the die has been cast.
Mom and Dad cannot help him,
he stands all alone.
A hit at this moment
would send the team home.
The ball meets the plate,
he swings and he misses.
There's a groan from the crowd,
with some boos and some hisses.
A thoughtless voice cries,
"Strike out the bum."
Tears fill his eyes,
the game's no longer fun.
So open your heart and give him a break,
For it's moments like this
a man you can make.
Please keep this in mind
when you hear someone forget.
He is just a little boy, and not a man yet.

Chaplain Bob Fox

Will You, Daddy?

It's strange, the things you remember. When life has crumbled suddenly, and left you standing there alone. It's not the big important things that you remember when you come to that, not the plans of years, not the love or the hopes you've worked so hard for. It's the little things that you remember then, the little things you hadn't noticed at the time. The way a hand touched yours, and you too busy to notice, the hopeful little inflection of a voice you didn't really bother to listen to.

John Carmody found that out, staring through the living-room window at the cheerful Tuesday afternoon life of the street. He kept trying to think about the big important things, lost now—the years and the plans, the hopes and the love. But he couldn't quite get them focused sharply in his mind just now—not this afternoon.

Those important things were like a huge nebulous background in his mind. All he could remember now was a queer little thing: nothing, really, if you stopped and thought about it in light of the years and the plans and the great love. It was only something his little girl had said to him one evening, two—perhaps three weeks ago. Nothing if you looked at it rationally—the sort of thing that kids are always saying.

But it was what he was remembering now.

That particular night, he had brought home from the office a finished draft of the annual stockholders' report. It was very important. Things being as they were, it meant a great deal to his future and to the futures of his wife and his little girl. He sat down to re-read it before dinner. It had to be right; it meant so much.

And just as he turned a page, Marge, his little girl, came with a book under her arm. It was a green-covered book, with a fairy tale picture pasted on it. She said, "Look, Daddy."

He glanced up and said, "Oh, fine. A new book, eh?"

"Yes, Daddy," she said. "Will you read me a story in it?"

"No, dear. Not just now," he said.

Marge just stood there as he read through a paragraph that told the stockholders about certain replacements in the machinery of the factory. And Marge's voice, with timid and hopeful little inflections, was saying, "But Mummy said you probably would, Daddy."

He looked up over the top of the typescript. "I'm sorry," he answered. "Maybe Mummy will read it to you. I'm busy, dear."

"No," Marge said politely, "Mummy is much busier upstairs. Won't you read me just this one story? Look, it has a picture. See? Isn't it a lovely picture, Daddy?"

"Oh, yes. Beautiful," he said, "Now that picture has class, hasn't it? But I do have to work tonight. Some other time . . ."

After that, there was quite a long silence. Marge just stood there with the book open at the lovely picture. It was a long time before she said anything else. He read through two more pages explaining in full detail, as he had directed, the shift in markets over the

past 12 months, the plans outlined by the sales
department for meeting these problems which, after
all, could safely be ascribed to local conditions, and
the advertising program that after weeks of confer-
ences had been devised to stabilize and even increase
the demand for their products.

"But it is a lovely picture, Daddy. And the story
looks so exciting," Marge said.

"I know," he said. "Ah . . . Mmmmm. Some other
time. Run along now."

"I'm sure you'd enjoy it, Daddy," Marge said.

"Eh? Yes, I know I would. But later . . ."

"Oh," Marge said. "Well, some other time then. Will
you, Daddy, some other time?"

"Oh, of course," he said. "You bet."

But she didn't go away. She still stood there quietly,
like a good child. And after a long time, she put the
book down on the stool at his feet and said, "Well,
whenever you get ready, just read it to yourself. Only
read it loud enough so I can hear, too."

"Sure," he said. "Sure—later."

And that was what John Carmody was remembering now, not the long plans of love and care for the
years ahead. He was remembering the way a well-
mannered child had touched his hand with timid little fingers and said, "Just read it to yourself. Only read
it loud enough so I can hear, too."

And that was why, now, he put his hand on the
book from the corner table, where they had piled
some of Marge's playthings, picking them up from
the floor where she had left them.

The book wasn't new anymore, and the green
cover was dented and thumbed. He opened it to the
lovely picture.

And reading that story, his lips moving stiffly with
anguish to form the words, he didn't try to think

anymore, as he should be thinking, about the important things, about his careful and shrewd and loving plans for the years to come, and for a little while he forgot, even, the horror and bitterness of his hate for the drunken driver who had careened down the street in a second-hand car, and who was now in jail on manslaughter charges.

He didn't even see his wife—white and silent—dressed to be with Marge for the last time, standing in the doorway, trying to make her voice say calmly, "I'm ready, dear. We must go."

Because John Carmody was reading:

"Once upon a time, there was a little girl who lived in a woodcutter's hut, in the Black Forest. And she was so fair that the birds forgot their singing from the bough, looking at her. And there came a day when . . ."

He was reading it to himself. But loud enough for her to hear, too. Maybe.

Michael Foster
Yunkster Gazette
Submitted by Martin Louw

But You Didn't

I looked at you and smiled the other day
I thought you'd see me but you didn't
I said "I love you" and waited for what you would say
I thought you'd hear me but you didn't
I asked you to come outside and play ball with me
I thought you'd follow me but you didn't
I drew a picture just for you to see
I thought you'd save it but you didn't
I made a fort for us back in the woods
I thought you'd camp with me but you didn't
I found some worms 'n such for fishing if we could
I thought you'd want to go but you didn't
I needed you just to talk to, my thoughts to share
I thought you'd want to but you didn't
I told you about the game hoping you'd be there
I thought you'd surely come but you didn't
I asked you to share my youth with me
I thought you'd want to but you couldn't
My country called me to war, you asked me
   to come home safely
But I didn't.

Stan Gebhardt

Graduation, Inheritance & Other Lessons

"It is with great pleasure that I present to you the 1978 graduating class of Drake University. These students have successfully completed their college studies: Michael M. Adams; congratulations, Michael. Margaret L. Allen; congratulations, Margaret."

He was so damn bullheaded! How could he *not* feel the torment of my urgency to go to college? How could he have possibly conjured up the idea that "if it's to be of meaning, it'll be accomplished on your own"? Damn him!

"John C. Anderson. Congratulations, John. Bettie J...."

One day he would see that I had done it on my own and he would feel remorse that he hadn't been a part of it, repentant and apologetic that he didn't actively follow me—freshman, sophomore, junior, senior . . . a college graduate.

". . . Burres. Congrat . . ."

There. I did it! I had made it through the vast land of ambiguity and bureaucratic hurdles. College—the test to measure your tolerance to stress! Four arduous years, and the prized sheepskin was mine. The scroll with my name inscribed on it confirmed it. Thanks a lot, Dad! I've longed for you to be supportive of me; to be proud of me; to think I was somebody special, really special. What happened to all those childhood lectures on accomplishing whatever you set your heart on? On principles, goals, work ethics and discipline? Where were the fatherly pats on my head along the way? What was so important that you couldn't tear yourself away to come to visit on parents day as all the other parents did?

And now, a no-show on graduation day. How could your day possibly be more consequential? How is it possible that you couldn't arrange your day to watch your daughter on this momentous event in her life?

" . . . ulations, Bettie."

Against all hope I searched for his eyes in the sea of several thousand faces in the audience. He was nowhere to be found. Naturally. My going off to college coincided with the birth of my parents' sixth child and other routines of a large and rural family. Why should he think of this day as anything out of the ordinary?

"Climb every mountain. Ford every stream." The song our graduation class had chosen for the theme seemed appropriately trite. And painful.

"Follow every rainbow . . . till you find your dream."

One hundred and two new graduates marched across the stage that day. I was sure that every one of them had two parents wedged in the crowded audience. When every graduate had picked up his or her diploma, our class rose and began the long march down the auditorium aisle, all of us ready to get out of sweaty gowns and prickly pins and rush off to the dinners and family graduation parties. I felt so alone. Saddened. Angry. I had sent Dad not one but two graduation invitations. It wasn't so much that I wanted him there, but that I needed him. Needed him to witness the completion of something very special, an outcome of all those dreams, ambitions and goals he had instilled in me. Didn't he know how much his approval of this meant to me? Were you serious, Dad, or was it just talk?

"Dad, you are coming, aren't you? I mean, how many times does one graduate from college?" I had pleaded.

"Our coming will depend on whether we're in the fields or not," he had said. "If it's a good planting day, we can't afford to miss it with the rains coming. We've missed so many days this spring. Planting time is critical now. *If* it rains, we'll *try* to make it down. But don't get your heart set on it. You know it's a two-hour drive to get there."

I did set my heart on it. It was all that mattered.

"Climb every mountain. Ford every . . ." Parents, grandparents and relatives were all smiles, straining for a glimpse of their new graduate, politely shoving others out of the way to get that cherished picture, proud of their own status as mother, father, grandparent, brother, sister, aunt, uncle *of the graduate*. Theirs were the tears of happiness; the tears I fought back were of absolute disappointment and rejection. It wasn't just that I felt alone, I was alone.

"Follow every rainbow . . ."

I had taken 27 steps from the spot where I had shaken hands with the University President in acceptance of my diploma—my ticket to the world in my future. "Bettie," a soft voice called urgently, startling me out of my suffocating invented dejection. The gentle sound of my father's voice leaked through the thunderous applause of an enormous, roaring audience. I'll never forget the vision that was before me. There in the end seat of the long aisle saved for the spillover of graduates, sat my father. He looked smaller and more reserved than the bold and thunderous man I grew up with. His eyes were red, and giant tears streamed down his cheeks, dropping thuds on a blue suit that was obviously brand new. His head was lowered slightly, and his face revealed a picture of far too many words. He looked so humble, too filled with fatherly pride. I'd seen him cry only one other time, but here were big quiet tears that couldn't be contained. The sight of this masculine and proud man—my father— in tears, broke the dam I had managed to hold back.

Within an instant, he was on his feet. My emotions under siege, I did what seemed like the thing to do in that fervent and impassioned moment—I thrust my diploma into his hand. "Here, this is for you," I said in a voice blended with love, arrogance, revenge, need, thanks and pride.

"This is for you," he countered in a voice devoid of anything but gentleness and love. His hand swiftly entered into his coat pocket and emerged with an envelope in it. In a clumsy gesture he reached out his weathered huge hand and thrust it at me. With the other hand, he rerouted the stream of tears cascading down his cheeks. It was the longest, most intense and emotional ten seconds I had participated in.

The procession continued. My heart raced as I tried to piece together the events of the day—his thoughts as he made the two-hour drive, his ease or frustration in finding the university, fending off graduates and hoarding a seat ten rows in front of those reserved for parents!

My dad had come! It was one of the most beautiful days the spring had to offer—a perfect planting day. And that new suit! As I remembered it, he had bought one for Uncle Ben's funeral. One decade later, he had purchased one for my sister's wedding. A suit was considered frivolous to this farmer; besides, owning one took away an excuse for not going where you didn't want to go! Buying a new suit definitely demanded a very important occasion. He was there;

Dad in his new suit.

"... till you find your dream."

I glanced at the envelope that I was crushing to death with my grip. Having never received a note or card from Dad before, I really didn't know what to think. My imagination went wild with the possibilities. Would it be a card ... with *his* signature? It was a rare and integrity-laden deal when E. H. Burres signed his name. Everyone knew a handshake from this man was better than a signature from someone else. When E. H. Burres gave his word—well, it was a done deal. No banker had ever turned down this man who after serving two terms in World War II had started his life with nothing more than a good work ethic, a solid sense of character, and a beautiful and loyal woman at his side; this man with all those kids and those bold dreams of owning all that land. Maybe it was just an extra copy of the graduation program. Maybe the exchange was just as flustering for him as it was for me and he simply handed me something, anything. Could it be an invitation to the assembling of the Burres clan to celebrate this day? Afraid of being let down, and wanting to savor any and all possibilities, I reserved opening the envelope until I reached the changing room. I struggled out of my cap and gown without letting go of this precious piece of paper.

"Look what my parents gave me for graduation," Martha gushed, as she held up her hand, showing off a gleaming pearl ring for all to see. "My old man gave me a car," yelled Todd from across the room. "Must be nice. I got nothing, as usual," came a voice from somewhere. "Yeah, me too!" chimed in another. "What did you get from your parents, Bettie?" yelled my college roommate from across the room.

It didn't seem appropriate to say, "Another incredible lesson, too precious to share, from one of the most admirable men in the world," so I turned away and pretended not to hear. I folded the graduation gown neatly and put it in a bag where it remains to this day—a symbol given life by my father's words and actions.

My eyes watered over as I remembered my father's tears. He had come after all. I was important to him. Either that or Mom won the fight! I opened the envelope slowly and carefully, not wanting to tear this precious memento from my father:

Dear Bettie,

I know you remember how as a young boy, my family had lost the family farm. My mother was left to raise six children, mostly alone. It was a rough time for all. On the day my family's farm was taken from us, I vowed that someday I would own land, and that all my children would have a legacy to this land. They would always be secure. Wherever they lived in the world, no matter what was to be their fate, there would always be a Burres homestead to come home to. My children would always have a home. The attached letter is your deed to your farm land. The taxes have been forever paid. It is yours.

When I saw you go off to college, you can imagine how proud I felt, and so hopeful that you would, one day, complete your degree. You can't really know how helpless I felt when I could not stretch our family's dollar to include your college. At the time, I didn't know how to say that without destroying your belief in me. But it wasn't because I didn't value what you were doing, nor was it for lack of recognition of how hard you were working to make your dream come true. Though I might not have followed you as closely as you would have liked, know that you were never out of my thoughts.

Always I watched you, though from afar. It might have seemed to you that I was impervious to your trials of going it alone, but I wasn't. I was coping with my own struggles of a growing family, and actualizing a dream I refused to let go of because it was so important to me—it was my legacy to you children.

I prayed for you constantly. Know, dear daughter, that your strength and ability to forge ahead when all seemed against you was often the very thing that kept my own dreams alive and renewed my strength to forge ahead with my own trials and tribulations—and made them worth it. You see, it was you who was my hero, a model of strength, courage and audacity.

There were times when you were home on holidays that as we walked the farmstead and talked about so many things, I wanted to tell you so you wouldn't lose faith in me. I needed you to believe in me. But as I watched the boundless energy of your youth and arrogance and pride, and listened to your determination to complete your mission, I knew you would be all right. I knew that not only could you do it, but that you would. And so, today we both have a piece of paper symbolizing the completion of dreams, actualized because we have applied hard work toward noble goals. Bettie, I am so very proud of you today.

Author's note: (His actual signature!)

— *Bettie B. Youngs*

My Father When I Was . . .

4 years old: My daddy can do anything.

5 years old: My daddy knows a whole lot.

6 years old: My dad is smarter than your dad.

8 years old: My dad doesn't know exactly everything.

10 years old: In the olden days when my dad grew up, things were sure different.

12 years old: Oh, well, naturally, Father doesn't know anything about that. He is too old to remember his childhood.

14 years old: Don't pay any attention to my father. He is so old-fashioned!

21 years old: Him? My Lord, he's hopelessly out-of-date.

25 years old: Dad knows a little bit about it, but then he should because he has been around so long.

30 years old: Maybe we should ask Dad what he thinks. After all, he's had a lot of experience.

35 years old: I'm not doing a single thing until I talk to Dad.

40 years old: I wonder how Dad would have handled it. He was so wise and had a world of experience.

50 years old: I'd give anything if Dad were here now so I could talk this over with him. Too bad I didn't appreciate how smart he was. I could have learned a lot from him.

Ann Landers

DENNIS THE MENACE By Ketcham

'Do you believe in yourself?'

DENNIS THE MENACE® used by permission of Hank Ketcham and
© by North America Syndicate.

The Spirit of Santa Doesn't Wear a Red Suit

I slouched down in the passenger seat of our old Pontiac 'cause it was the cool way to sit when one is in the fourth grade. My dad was driving downtown to shop and I was going along for the ride. At least that's what I had told him—actually I had an important question to ask that had been on my mind for a couple of weeks and this was the first time I had been able to maneuver myself into his presence without being overt about it.

"Dad . . . " I started. And stopped.

"Yup?" he said.

"Some of the kids at school have been saying something and I know it's not true." I felt my lower lip quiver from the effort of trying to hold back the tears I felt threatening the inside corner of my right eye—it was always the one that wanted to cry first.

"What is it, Punkin?" I knew he was in a good mood when he used this endearment.

"The kids say there is no Santa Claus." Gulp. One tear escaped. "They say I'm dumb to believe in Santa anymore . . . it's only for little kids." My left eye started with a tear on the inside track.

"But I believe what you told me. That Santa is real. He is, isn't he, Dad?"

Up to this point we had been cruising down Newell Avenue, which was in those days a two-lane road lined with oak trees. At my question, my dad glanced over at my face and body position. He pulled over to the side of the road and stopped the car. Dad turned off the engine and moved over closer to me, his still-little girl huddled in the corner.

"The kids at school are wrong, Patty. Santa Claus is real."

"I knew it!" I heaved a sigh of relief.

"But there is more I need to tell you about Santa. I think you are old enough now to understand what I am going to share with you. Are you ready?" My dad had a warm gleam in his eyes and a soft expression on his face. I knew something big was up and I was ready 'cause I trusted him completely. He would never lie to me.

"Once upon a time there was a real man who traveled the world and gave away presents to deserving children everywhere he went. You will find him in many lands with different names, but what he had in his heart was the same in every language. In America we call him Santa Claus. He is the spirit of unconditional love and the desire to share that love by giving presents from the heart. When you get to a certain age, you come to realize that the real Santa Claus is not the guy who comes down your chimney on Christmas Eve. The real life and spirit of this magical elf lives forever in your heart, my heart, Mom's heart and in the hearts and minds of all people who believe in the joy that giving to others brings. The real spirit of Santa becomes what you can give rather than what you get. Once you understand this and it becomes a part of you, Christmas becomes even more exciting and more magical because you come to realize the magic comes from you when Santa lives in your heart.

Do you understand what I am trying to tell you?"

I was gazing out the front window with all my concentration at a tree in front of us. I was afraid to look
at my dad—the person who had told me all of my life
that Santa was a real being. I wanted to believe like I
believed last year—that Santa was a big fat elf in a red
suit. I did not want to swallow the grow-up pill and
see anything different.

"Patty, look at me." My dad waited. I turned my
head and looked at him.

Dad had tears in his eyes, too—tears of joy. His face
shone with the light of a thousand galaxies and I saw
in his eyes the eyes of Santa Claus. The real Santa
Claus. The one who spent time choosing special
things I had wanted for all the Christmases past since
the time I had come to live on this planet. The Santa
who ate my carefully decorated cookies and drank
the warm milk. The Santa who probably ate the car-
rot I left for Rudolf. The Santa who—despite his utter
lack of mechanical skills—put together bicycles, wag-
ons and other miscellaneous items during the wee
hours of Christmas mornings.

I got it. I got the joy, the sharing, the love. My dad
pulled me to him in a warm embrace and just held
me for what seemed like the longest time. We both
cried.

"Now you belong to a special group of people," Dad
continued. "You will share in the joy of Christmas from
now on, every day of the year, not only on a special
day. For now, Santa Claus lives in your heart just like
he lives in mine. It is your responsibility to fulfill the
spirit of giving as your part of Santa living inside of
you. This is one of the most important things that can
happen to you in your whole life, because now you
know that Santa Claus cannot exist without people
like you and me to keep him alive. Do you think you

can handle it?"

My heart swelled with pride and I'm sure my eyes were shining with excitement. "Of course, Dad. I want him to be in my heart, just like he's in yours. I love you, Daddy. You're the best Santa there ever was in the whole world."

When it comes time in my life to explain the reality of Santa Claus to my children, I pray to the spirit of Christmas that I will be as eloquent and loving as my dad was the day I learned that the spirit of Santa Claus doesn't wear a red suit. And I hope they will be as receptive as I was that day. I trust them totally and I think they will.

Patty Hansen

The Little Lady Who Changed My Life

She was four years old when I first met her. She was carrying a bowl of soup. She had very, very fine golden hair and a little pink shawl around her shoulders. I was 29 at the time and suffering from the flu. Little did I realize that this little lady was going to change my life.

Her mom and I had been friends for many years. Eventually that friendship grew into care, from care into love, to marriage, and marriage brought the three of us together as a family. At first I was awkward because in the back of my mind, I thought I would be stuck with the dreaded label of "stepfather." And stepfathers were somehow mythically, or in a real sense, ogres as well as an emotional wedge in the special relationship between the child and the biological father.

Early on I tried hard to make a natural transition from bachelorhood to fatherhood. A year and a half before we married, I took an apartment a few blocks away from their home. When it became evident that we would marry, I tried to spend time to enable a smooth changeover from friend to father figure. I tried not to become a wall between my future daughter and her natural father. Still, I longed to be something special in her life.

Over the years, my appreciation for her grew. Her honesty, sincerity and directness were mature beyond her years. I knew that within this child lived a very giving and compassionate adult. Still, I lived in the fear that some day, when I had to step in and be a disciplinarian, I might have it thrown in my face that I wasn't her "real" father. If I wasn't real, why would she have to listen to me? My actions became measured. I was probably more lenient than I wanted to be. I acted in that way in order to be liked, all the time living out a role I felt I had to live—thinking I wasn't good enough or worthy enough on my own terms.

During the turbulent teenage years, we seemed to drift apart emotionally. I seemed to lose control (or at least the parental illusion of control). She was searching for her identity and so was I. I found it increasingly hard to communicate with her. I felt a sense of loss and sadness because I was getting further from the feeling of oneness we had shared so easily in the beginning.

Because she went to a parochial school, there was an annual retreat for all seniors. Evidently the students thought that going on retreat was like a week at Club Med. They boarded the bus with their guitars and racquetball gear. Little did they realize that this was going to be an emotional encounter that could have a lasting impression on them. As parents of the participants, we were asked to individually write a letter to our child, being open and honest and to write only positive things about our relationship. I wrote a letter about the little golden-haired girl who had brought me a bowl of soup when I needed care. During the course of the week, the students delved deeper into their real beings. They had an opportunity to read the letters we parents had prepared for them.

The parents also got together one night during that week to think about and send good thoughts to our children. While she was away, I noticed something come out of me that I knew was there all along, but which I hadn't faced. It was that in order to be fully appreciated I had to plainly be me. I didn't have to act like anyone else. I wouldn't be overlooked if I was true to myself. I just had to be the best me I could be. It may not sound like much to anyone else, but it was one of the biggest revelations of my life.

The night arrived when they came home from their retreat experience. The parents and friends who had come to pick them up were asked to arrive early, and then invited into a large room where the lights were turned down low. Only the lights in the front of the room were shining brightly.

The students marched joyously in, all dirty-faced as though they had just come back from summer camp. They filed in arm-in-arm, singing a song they had designated as their theme for the week. Through their smudgy faces, they radiated a new sense of belonging and love and self-confidence.

When the lights were turned on, the kids realized that their parents and friends, who had come to collect them and share their joy, were also in the room. The students were allowed to make a few statements about their perceptions of the prior week. At first they reluctantly got up and said things like, "It was cool," and "Awesome week," but after a few moments you could begin to see a real vitality in the students' eyes. They began to reveal things that underscored the importance of this rite of passage. Soon they were straining to get to the microphone. I noticed my daughter was anxious to say something. I was equally anxious to hear what she had to say.

I could see my daughter determinedly inching her way up to the microphone. Finally she got to the front of the line. She said something like, "I had a great time, and I learned a lot about myself." She continued, "I want to say there are people and things we sometimes take for granted that we shouldn't, and I just want to say . . . I love you, Tony."

At that moment my knees got weak. I had no expectations, no anticipation she would say anything so heartfelt. Immediately people around me started hugging me, and patting me on the back as though they also understood the depth of that remarkable statement. For a teenage girl to say openly in front of a room full of people, "I love you," took a great deal of courage. If there were something greater than being overwhelmed, I was experiencing it.

Since then the magnitude of our relationship has increased. I have come to understand and appreciate that I didn't need to have any fear about being a step-father. I only have to concern myself with being the real person who can exchange honest love with the same little girl I met so many years before—carrying a bowl full of what turned out to be kindness.

Tony Luna

10th Row Center

A man came up and introduced himself to me after one of my seminars in Detroit, Michigan. He said, "Mr. Rohn, you got me tonight. I've decided to change my whole life."

I said, "Fantastic!"

He said, "You will hear about it someday."

I said, "I don't doubt that."

Sure enough, a few months later I was back in Detroit for another lecture and the same man walked up and said, "Mr. Rohn, do you remember me?"

I said, "I do. You are the man who said he was going to change his life." "That's me," he said. "I've got to tell you a story. After the last seminar, I started thinking about ways to begin changing my life and I decided to start with my family. I have two lovely daughters— the best kids anyone could ask for. They never give me any trouble. However, I've always given them a hard time—especially as teenagers. One of the things they dearly love to do is go to rock-and-roll concerts to see their favorite performers. Now, I've always given them a hard time on this subject. They would ask to go and I would always say, 'No, the music is too loud, you'll ruin your hearing and it's the wrong kind of crowd to be in.'

"Then, they would beg, 'Please Daddy, we want to

go. We don't give you any trouble. We're good girls. Please let us go.'

"Well, after they had begged long enough, I would reluctantly throw them the money and say, 'Okay, if you have to go that bad.' So that's where I decided to make some changes in my life." Then he said, "Here's what I did. Not long ago I saw this advertisement that one of their favorite performers was coming to town. Guess what I did? I went down to the concert hall and bought the tickets myself. Later that day, when I saw my girls, I handed them the envelope and said, 'Daughters of mine, you may not believe this—but inside this envelope are your tickets to the concert that's coming to town.' They could not believe it. Then I told them one more thing. I said, 'Your begging days are over.' Now my girls really couldn't believe it. Finally, I made them promise not to open the envelope until they got to the concert, and they agreed. Now comes concert time. When the girls arrived, they opened the envelope and handed the tickets to the usher who said, 'Follow me.' As he guided them toward the front, the girls said, ' Wait a minute. Something must be wrong.' The usher then looked at the tickets, and said, 'There's nothing wrong. Follow me.' Finally they get down to 10th row center. The girls were astonished. I stayed up a little late that night, and sure enough around midnight my daughters came bursting through the front door. One of them landed in my lap. The other one had her arms around my neck. And they both said, 'Dad, you've got to be one of the world's all-time great fathers!'"

What a great example of how it is possible, with just a change in attitude and a little thought, to live the good life.

Jim Rohn

The Annual Letters

Shortly after my daughter Juli-Ann was born, I started a loving tradition that I know others (with whom I have subsequently shared this special plan) have also started. I tell you the idea here both to open your heart with the warmth of my story and also to encourage you to start this tradition within your own family.

Every year, on her birthday, I write an Annual Letter to my daughter. I fill it with funny anecdotes that happened to her that year, hardships or joys, issues that are important in my life or hers, world events, my predictions for the future, miscellaneous thoughts, etc. I add to the letter photographs, presents, report cards and many other types of mementos that would certainly have otherwise disappeared as the years passed.

I keep a folder in my desk drawer in which, all year long, I place things that I want to include in the envelope containing her next Annual Letter. Every week, I make short notes of what I can think of from the week's events that I will want to recall later in the year to write in her Annual Letter. When her birthday approaches, I take out that folder and find it overflowing with ideas, thoughts, poems, cards, treasures, stories, incidents and memories of all sorts—many of which I had already forgotten—and which I then eagerly transcribe into that year's Annual Letter.

Once the letter is written and all the treasures are inserted into the envelope, I seal it. It then becomes that year's Annual Letter. On the envelope I always write "Annual Letter to Juli-Ann from her Daddy on the occasion of her *nth* Birthday—to be opened when she is 21 years old."

It is a time capsule of love from every different year of her life, to her as an adult. It is a gift of loving memories from one generation to the next. It is a permanent record of her life, written as she was actually living it.

Our tradition is that I show her the sealed envelope, with the proclamation written on it that she may read it when she is 21. Then I take her to the bank, open the safe deposit box and tenderly place that year's Annual Letter on top of the growing pile of its predecessors. She sometimes takes them all out to look at them and feel them. She sometimes asks me about their contents and I always refuse to tell her what is inside.

In recent years, Juli-Ann has given me some of her special childhood treasures, which she is growing too old for but which she does not want to lose. And she asks me to include them in her Annual Letter so that she will always have them.

That tradition of writing her Annual Letters is now one of my most sacred duties as a dad. And, as Juli-Ann grows older, I can see that it is a growing and special part of her life, too.

One day, we were sitting with friends musing about what we will be doing in the future. I cannot recall the exact words spoken, but it went something like this: I jokingly told Juli-Ann that on her 61st birthday, she will be playing with her grandchildren.

Then, I whimsically invented that on her 31st birthday she will be driving her own kids to hockey practice. Getting into the groove of this funny game and encouraged by Juli-Ann's evident enjoyment of my fantasies, I continued. On your 21st birthday, you will be graduating from university. "No," she interjected. "I will be too busy reading!"

One of my deepest desires is to be alive and present to enjoy that wonderful time in the future when the time capsules are opened and the accumulated mountains of love come tumbling out of the past, back into my adult daughter's life.

Raymond L. Aaron

The Baggy Yellow Shirt

The baggy yellow shirt had long sleeves, four extra-large pockets trimmed in black thread and snaps up the front. Not terribly attractive, but utilitarian without a doubt. I found it in December 1963 during my freshman year in college when I was home on Christmas break.

Part of the fun of vacation at home was the chance to go through Mom's hoard of rummage, destined for the less fortunate. She regularly scoured the house for clothes, bedding and housewares to give away, and the collection was always stored in paper bags on the floor of the front hall closet.

Looking through Mom's collection one day, I came across this oversized yellow shirt, slightly faded from years of wear but still in decent shape.

"Just the thing to wear over my clothes during art class!" I said to myself.

"You're not taking that old thing, are you?" Mom said when she saw me packing it. "I wore that when I was pregnant with your brother in 1954!"

"It's perfect for art class, Mom. Thanks!" I slipped it into my suitcase before she could object.

The yellow shirt became a part of my college wardrobe. I loved it. All during college, it stayed with me, always comfortable to throw over my clothes during messy projects. The underarm seams had to be reinforced before I graduated, but there was plenty of wear in that old garment.

After graduation I moved to Denver and wore the

shirt the day I moved into my apartment. Then I wore it on Saturday mornings when I cleaned. Those four large pockets on the front—two breast pockets and two at hip level—made a super place to carry dust cloths, wax and polish.

The next year, I married. When I became pregnant, I found the yellow shirt tucked in a drawer and wore it during those big-belly days. Though I missed sharing my first pregnancy with Mom and Dad and the rest of my family, since we were in Colorado and they were in Illinois, that shirt helped remind me of their warmth and protection. I smiled and hugged the shirt when I remembered that Mother had worn it when she was pregnant.

By 1969, after my daughter's birth, the shirt was at least 15 years old. That Christmas, I patched one elbow, washed and pressed the shirt, wrapped it in holiday paper and sent it to Mom. Smiling, I tucked a note in one of the pockets saying: "I hope this fits. I'm sure it will look great on you!" When Mom wrote to thank me for her "real" gifts, she said the yellow shirt was lovely. She never mentioned it again.

The next year, my husband, daughter and I moved from Denver to St. Louis and we stopped at Mom and Dad's house in Rock Falls, Illinois, to pick up some furniture. Days later, when we uncrated the kitchen table, I noticed something yellow taped to its bottom. The shirt! And so the pattern was set.

On our next visit home, I secretly placed the shirt between the mattress and box springs of Mom and Dad's bed. I don't know how long it took her to find it, but almost two years passed before I got it back.

By then our family had grown.

This time Mom got even with me. She put it under the base of our living-room lamp, knowing that as a mother of three little ones, housecleaning and moving lamps would not be everyday events.

When I finally got the shirt, I wore it often while refinishing "early marriage" furniture that I found at rummage sales. The walnut stains on the shirt simply added more character to all its history.

Unfortunately, our lives were full of stains, too.

My marriage had been failing almost from the beginning. After a number of attempts at marriage counseling, my husband and I divorced in 1975. The three children and I prepared to move back to Illinois to be closer to the emotional support of family and friends.

As I packed, a deep depression overtook me. I wondered if I could make it on my own with three small children to raise. I wondered if I would find a job. Although I hadn't read the Bible much since my Catholic school days, I paged through the Good Book, looking for comfort. In Ephesians, I read, "So use every piece of God's armor to resist the enemy whenever he attacks, and when it is all over, you will be standing up."

I tried to picture myself wearing God's armor, but all I saw was me wearing the stained yellow shirt. Of course! Wasn't my mother's love a piece of God's armor? I smiled and remembered the fun and warm feelings the yellow shirt had brought into my life over the years. My courage was renewed and somehow the future didn't seem so alarming.

Unpacking in our new home and feeling much better, I knew I had to get the shirt back to Mother. The next time I visited her, I carefully tucked it in her bottom dresser drawer, knowing that sweater weather was months away.

Meanwhile my life moved splendidly. I found a good job at a radio station and the children thrived in their new environment.

A year later during a window-washing spurt, I found the crumpled yellow shirt hidden in a rag bag in my cleaning closet. Something new had been added. Emblazoned across the top of the breast pocket were the bright green newly embroidered words, "I BELONG TO PAT." Not to be outdone, I got out my own embroidery materials and added an apostrophe and seven more letters. Now the shirt proudly proclaimed, "I BELONG TO PAT'S MOTHER."

Once again, I zigzagged all the frayed seams. Then I enlisted the aid of a dear friend, Harold, to help me get it back to Mom. He arranged to have a friend mail the shirt to Mom from Arlington, Virginia. We enclosed a letter announcing that she was the recipient of an award for her good deeds. The award letter, on official-looking stationery printed at the high school where Harold was assistant principal, came from "The Institute for the Destitute."

This was my finest hour. I would have given anything to see Mom's face when she opened the "award" box and saw the shirt inside. But, of course, she never mentioned it.

On Easter Sunday the following year, Mother managed a coup de grace. She walked into our home with regal poise, wearing that old shirt over her Easter outfit, as if it were an integral part of her wardrobe.

I'm sure my mouth hung open, but I said nothing. During the Easter meal, a giant laugh choked my throat. But I was determined not to break the unbroken spell the shirt had woven into our lives. I was sure that Mom would take off the shirt and try to hide it in my home, but when she and Dad left, she walked out the door wearing, "I BELONG TO PAT'S MOTHER" like a coat of arms.

A year later, in June 1978, Harold and I were married. The day of our wedding, we hid our car in a friend's garage to avoid the usual practical jokers. After the wedding, while my husband drove us to our honeymoon suite in Wisconsin, I reached for a pillow in the car so I could rest my head. The pillow felt lumpy. I unzipped the case and discovered a gift, wrapped in wedding paper.

I thought it might be a surprise gift from Harold. But he looked as stunned as I. Inside the box was the freshly pressed yellow shirt.

Mother knew I'd need the shirt as a reminder that a sense of humor, spiced with love, is one of the most important ingredients in a happy marriage. In a pocket was a note: "Read John 14:27-29. I love you both, Mother."

That night I paged through a Bible I found in the hotel room and found the verses: "I am leaving you with a gift: peace of mind and heart. And the peace I give isn't fragile like the peace the world gives. So don't be troubled or afraid. Remember what I told you: I am going away, but I will come back to you again. If you really love me, you will be very happy for me, for now I can go to the Father, who is greater than I am. I have told you these things before they happen so that when they do, you will believe in me."

The shirt was Mother's final gift.

She had known for three months before my wedding that she had a terminal disease, amyotrophic lateral sclerosis (Lou Gehrig's disease). Mother died 13 months later, at age 57. I must admit that I was tempted to send the yellow shirt with her to her grave. But I'm glad I didn't, because it is a vivid reminder of the love-filled game she and I played for 16 years.

Besides, my older daughter is in college now, majoring in art . . . and every art student needs a baggy yellow shirt with big pockets for art class!

Patricia Lorenz

The Gift

"Grandpa, please come," I said, knowing he wouldn't. In the pale light that filtered through the dusty kitchen window, he sat stiffly in his padded vinyl chair, his thick arms resting on the Formica table, staring past me at the wall. He was a gruff, crusty, old-country Italian, with a long memory for past hurts both real and imagined. When he was feeling testy, he responded with a grunt. He gave me one now that meant no.

"Come on, Gramps," pleaded my six-year-old sister, Carrie. "I want you to come." Twenty-one years younger than I, she had been a startlingly late addition to our family. "I'm going to make your favorite cookies just for you. Mommy said she would show me."

"It's for Thanksgiving, for God's sake," I said. "You haven't joined us for dinner for four years now. Don't you think it's about time we let the past be?"

He glanced at me, his blue eyes flashing the same fierce intensity that had intimidated the entire family all these years. Except me. Somehow, I knew him. Perhaps I shared more of his loneliness than I cared to admit, and the same inability to let emotions show. Whatever the reason, I knew what was inside him. *The sins of the fathers will be visited on their sons*, it was written, and so they were. How much suffering occurs because of the unfortunate "gift" each male receives before he is old enough to decide if he wants it, this misguided idea of manhood. We end up hard on the outside, helpless on the inside, and the few feet that separated me from my grandfather might just as well have been measured in light years.

Carrie chattered on, still trying to convince him. She had no idea how hopeless it was.

I got up and walked to the window overlooking his backyard. In the winter light, the disheveled garden was a delicate gray, overgrown with tangled weeds and vines gone wild. Grandpa used to work miracles there—a substitute, perhaps, for his inability to orchestrate his own nature. But after Grandma died, he let the garden go, retreating even further into himself.

Turning away from the window, I studied him in the deepening gloom. From his prominent chin to his thick, rough hands, everything about him reflected the relentless discipline his life had been: work since age 13, the humiliation of unemployment during the Depression, decades of hard manual labor in the Trenton Stone Quarry. Not an easy life.

I kissed him on the cheek. "We have to go now, Grandpa. I'll pick you up if you decide to come."

He sat stone-still, staring straight ahead, sucking on his old pipe.

A few days later, Carrie asked me for Grandpa's address.

"What for?" I asked.

She was neatly folding a sheet of paper to fit into a blue envelope. "I want to send him a gift. I made it myself."

I told her the address, pausing after each line so she could get it all down. She wrote slowly, concentrating on making each letter and number neat and round. When she finished, she put her pencil down and said firmly, "I want to mail it myself. Will you take me to the mailbox?"

"We'll do it later, okay?"

"I need to do it now. Please?"

So we did.

On Thanksgiving I awoke late to the delicious smell of pasta sauce. Mom was preparing her special dinner of ravioli, turkey, broccoli, sweet potatoes, and cranberry sauce, a wonderful amalgam of Italian and American traditions. "We need only four places, Carrie," she was saying as I entered the kitchen.

Carrie shook her head. "No, Mommy, we need five. Gramps is going to come."

"Oh, honey," Mom said.

"He's coming," my sister said flatly. "I know he is."

"Carrie, give us a break. He isn't coming and you know it," I said. I didn't want to see her day spoiled by crushing disappointment.

"John, let her be." Mom looked at Carrie. "Set an extra place then."

Dad came in from the living room. He stood in the doorway, hands in his pockets, looking at Carrie as she set the table.

Finally we sat down to dinner. For a moment we were all silent. Then, glancing at Carrie, Mom said, "I guess we had better say grace now. Carrie?"

My sister looked toward the door. Then she set her chin, bowed her head and mumbled, "Please bless us, O Lord, and the food we are about to eat. And bless Grandpa . . . and help him to hurry. Thank you, God."

Shooting glances at each other, we sat in silence, no one willing to seal Grandpa's absence and disappoint Carrie by eating. The clock ticked in the hallway.

Suddenly there was a muffled knocking at the door. Carrie leapt to her feet and ran down the hallway. She tore open the door. "Gramps!"

He stood straight in his black, shiny suit, the only one he owned, pressing a black fedora against his chest with one hand and dangling a brown paper bag with the other. "I bring squash," he said, holding up the bag.

Several months later, Grandpa died quietly in his sleep. Cleaning out his dresser, I found a blue envelope, a folded piece of paper inside. It was a child's drawing of our kitchen table with five chairs around it. One of the chairs was empty, the others occupied by faded stick figures labeled Momy, Dady, Johny and Carrie. Hearts were drawn on the four of us, each cracked jaggedly down the middle.

John Catenacci

She Remembered

My mother is the sweetest, most kind-hearted person you would ever want to meet. She was always very bright and articulate, and would do anything for anyone. We've always had a close and special relationship. She is also someone whose brain is being ravaged and whose identity is being stripped away slowly because of Alzheimer's disease. She has been slipping away from us for 10 years now. For me, it is a constant death, a slow letting go and a continual grieving process. Although she had lost almost all ability to care for herself, she at least still knew her immediate family. I knew the day would come when that, too, would change and finally, about two-and-a-half years ago, that day came.

My parents would visit us almost daily and we would have a pleasant time, but suddenly there was a connection missing. My mother no longer knew me as her daughter. She would tell my father, "Oh, they are such nice people." Telling her I was her daughter made no difference at all. I had now joined the ranks of a "nice neighbor." When I would hug her good-bye, I would close my eyes and imagine that this was my mother from years ago. I would drink in every familiar sensation that I have known for 36 years—her warm comforting body, the squeeze of her arms and the soft, sweet smell that was hers alone.

This part of the disease was difficult for me to accept and deal with. I was going through a rough time in my life and particularly felt the need for my mother. I prayed for us both and about how much I needed her.

One late summer afternoon while I was preparing dinner, my prayers were answered and I was taken by surprise. My parents and husband were outside on the patio when my mother suddenly jumped up as if hit by a bolt of lightning. She ran into the kitchen, grabbed me gently from behind and turned me around. With a deep sense of knowledge in her eyes that seemed to transcend time and space, she tearfully and with great emotion asked me if it was true, was I her baby? Overwhelmed with emotion, I cried, yes, it was true. We hugged and cried and neither of us wanted to let go of this magical moment. I knew it could disappear as quickly as it came. She said she felt a closeness to me and that I was a nice person, but that it had come to her suddenly that I was her child. We felt relief and joy. I took this gift from God and savored it, even if it were to last just for that moment or hour or day. We were given a reprieve from that awful disease and we had a special connection again. There was a sparkle back in her eyes that had been gone for a long time.

Although my mother's condition has continued to deteriorate, she remembers who I am and it has been a year since that sweet summer afternoon. She gives me a special look and smile that seems to say, "We are in on a secret that no one else knows about." A few months ago when she was here and we had another visitor, she started stroking my hair and told them proudly, "Did you know that she was my baby?"

Lisa Boyd

Rescued

A little girl whose parents had died lived with her grandmother and slept in an upstairs bedroom.

One night there was a fire in the house and the grandmother perished while trying to rescue the child. The fire spread quickly, and the first floor of the house was soon engulfed in flames.

Neighbors called the fire department, then stood helplessly by, unable to enter the house because flames blocked all the entrances. The little girl appeared at an upstairs window, crying for help, just as word spread among the crowd that firefighters would be delayed a few minutes because they were all at another fire.

Suddenly, a man appeared with a ladder, put it up against the side of the house and disappeared inside. When he reappeared, he had the little girl in his arms. He delivered the child to the waiting arms below, then disappeared into the night.

An investigation revealed that the child had no living relatives, and weeks later a meeting was held in the town hall to determine who would take the child into their home and bring her up.

A teacher said she would like to raise the child. She pointed out that she could ensure a good education. A farmer offered her an upbringing on his farm. He pointed out that living on a farm was healthy and satisfying. Others spoke, giving their reasons why it was to the child's advantage to live with them.

Finally, the town's richest resident arose and said, "I can give this child all the advantages that you have mentioned here, plus money and everything that money can buy."

Throughout all this, the child remained silent, her eyes on the floor.

"Does anyone else want to speak?" asked the meeting chairman. A man came forward from the back of the hall. His gait was slow and he seemed in pain. When he got to the front of the room, he stood directly before the little girl and held out his arms. The crowd gasped. His hand and arms were terribly scarred.

The child cried out, "This is the man who rescued me!" With a leap, she threw her arms around the man's neck, holding on for dear life, just as she had that fateful night. She buried her face in his shoulder and sobbed for a few moments. Then she looked up and smiled at him.

"This meeting is adjourned," said the chairman.

Author Unknown

Little Eyes Upon You

There are little eyes upon you
and they're watching night and day.
There are little ears that quickly
take in every word you say.
There are little hands all eager
to do anything you do;
And a little boy who's dreaming
of the day he'll be like you.

You're the little fellow's idol,
you're the wisest of the wise.
In his little mind about you
no suspicions ever rise.
He believes in you devoutly,
holds all you say and do;
He will say and do, in your way
when he's grown up just like you.

There's a wide-eyed little fellow
who believes you're always right;
and his eyes are always opened,
and he watches day and night.
You are setting an example
every day in all you do;
For the little boy who's waiting
to grow up to be like you.

Author Unknown
Submitted by Ronald Dahlsten

3

ON DEATH AND DYING

*D*eath is a challenge.
It tells us not to waste time . . .
It tells us to tell each other right
now that we love each other.

Leo F. Buscaglia

Go Into the Light

Until about six years ago, the most unique commodity in Gilroy, California was garlic; and then a little angel was born. Shannon Brace was a miracle baby born to her mother, Laurie, who had been told years before that she could never have children. She had been carrying twins for three-and-a-half months when one of the twins died. Little Shannon then showed her first courageous signs of never giving up and held on for life. Shannon was diagnosed at age two-and-a-half with cancer. Her doctors said she would not live long, but with love and determination she lived a couple more years.

At one point, doctors needed to harvest bone marrow from her pelvic bone. Shannon had an endodermal sinus tumor, or germ cell cancer. Only 75 out of 7,500 children who get cancer each year are diagnosed with germ cell cancer.

Shannon experienced two years of chemotherapy before she had a bone marrow transplant. It is a life-threatening operation with an unsure outcome. An autologous bone marrow transplant along with a near-lethal dose of chemotherapy kept her teetering along the path of life and death.

She was told she would never walk after chemotherapy and she would be paralyzed. She did walk, although she weighed only 27 pounds. Laurie said, "The will these children have is incredible." Her courage was astounding even up to the end, with a vivacious commitment to never give up. Shannon received a trophy at a Santa Clara beauty pageant, an award for courage.

Shannon's father, Larry, was disabled from a motorcycle accident that broke his back, neck and both legs—around the same time Shannon's disease was discovered. Larry, who stayed home during the day with Shannon, says, "She had the strongest will to live. She wanted to prove people wrong."

Laurie explains that her family lives on hope. You'd never know that Shannon understood she was dying by watching her. She was always full of enthusiasm, love and an overwhelming concern for others around her. During Shannon's stay at Stanford Medical Center, she lost more best friends in a few short years to death than most elderly people do in a lifetime.

During one of Shannon's more sober moments, she awoke at night, sat up straight and, holding her parents tight, she asked her mother not to make her go to heaven. Laurie responded with her voice breaking, "God, how I wish I could promise you."

Sometimes she was even a little stinker. In a grocery store one day with her mother, a friendly man decided to be humorous as he said, "You sure shaved his head close!" Not meaning to offend, Shannon responded, "You know, sir, I am a little girl and I have cancer and I might die."

One morning with Shannon coughing excessively, her mom said, "We'll have to go to Stanford again."

"No, I'm okay," Shannon piped up.

"I think we need to go, Shannon."

"No, I only have a cold."

"Shannon we need to go!"

"Okay, but only for three days or I'm hitchhiking home."

Shannon's perseverance and optimism afforded her a full life to those who were blessed to surround her.

Shannon's life was concentrated outside of herself and her needs. At times when she would be lying in a hospital bed very ill, she would often jump up to assist a roommate upon hearing of their needs.

Another day, seeing a stranger walking by their home looking very sad, she ran outside, handed him a flower and wished him a happy day.

And on another occasion, as Shannon was lying in the Stanford Children's Hospital one Friday afternoon, moans slipped past her lips as she held her favorite, but worn, blankie. Coming out of anesthesia, she alternated hiccups and sobs. Again, she pushed past her needs as she inquired to the well-being of those around her.

One of her first questions was to her mother just as her eyelids were opening: "How you doing?"

"I'm fine, Shannie," said her mom, "How are you?"

As soon as her hiccups and cries passed, she said, "I'm okay."

Shannon got directly involved in local fund-raisers, as their family's insurance wouldn't cover her treatment. She walked into a Gilroy cannery and walked up to the first person she saw and began carrying on a conversation. She was full of light and love for everyone. She never noticed differences between people. She eventually said, "I have cancer and I might die." Later, when this same man was asked if he would donate tin cans from his cannery to Shannon's cause, he said, "Give her anything she wants, including a business card."

Shannon's mother, Laurie, summarizes Shannon

and other terminally ill children in the following way: "They take every bit of life and pull it out to the end. They are not important anymore; it is the world around them that is important."

At age four, as little angel Shannon was hovering between life and death, her family knew it was her time to go. Gathering around her bedside, they encouraged her to walk toward the tunnel of light. Shannon responded, "It's too bright." Encouraged to walk toward the angels, she replied, "They are singing too loud."

If you were to walk by little Shannon's headstone at the Gilroy cemetery, you would read this from her family: "May you always walk hand in hand with the other angels. There is nothing in this world that will ever change our love."

On October 10, 1991, the *Dispatch*, Gilroy's local newspaper, ran this letter that 12-year-old Damien Codara wrote to his friend Shannon before she died:

Go to the light, Shannon, where those who have gone before you wait, with anticipation of feeling your presence. They will welcome you with open arms, combined with love, laughter and feelings that are the happiest that could be possibly felt by anyone, on earth or in heaven. Shannon, there is no pain or suffering. Sadness is an absolute impossibility. When you enter the light you can play with all of your friends that mysteriously disappeared while you were so gallantly battling the evil plague of cancer, and dodging cleverly the Grim Reaper's angry hand of the darkness that he possesses.

Those that are still on earth will certainly miss you deeply and long for your sense of specialness, but you will live in our hearts and spirits. You are the reason that all people who knew you were somehow brought closer to each other.

What is truly amazing is the way that, no matter what problems or complicated obstacles you had confront you, you consistently overpowered and overcame every one of them. However, sadly the final confrontation overcame you. Instead of thinking that you gave up, we admire your braveness and gallantry. We are somewhat relieved that you are finally going to feel the freedom of being a regular little girl and know that you've probably accomplished more than most of us will ever accomplish.

The hearts you've touched will never lose the feeling of love. So, Shannon, when you suddenly find yourself alone in a dark tunnel and a pinpoint of light is visible, remember us, Shannie, and find the courage to go into the light.

Donna Loesch

Suki . . . A Best Friend
for All Reasons

As a small child, I could not understand
why I should pray for human beings only.
When my mother had kissed me goodnight,
I used to add a silent prayer that I had com-
posed for all living creatures.

Albert Schweitzer

The first time I saw her she was sitting in the midst of several jumping, yapping dogs who were all trying to get my attention. With quiet dignity, she gazed at me with her huge brown eyes, soft and liquid with a knowing that transported both of us far beyond the animal shelter. Her eyes were her best feature. The rest of her seemed to have been put together by someone with a great sense of humor and access to many different kinds of dogs. The head of a dachshund, spots of a terrier, legs seen better on a Welsh corgi and the tail of perhaps . . . a Doberman pinscher? All in all she was an amazing sight . . . the ugliest dog I had ever seen.

I named her Suki Sue Shaw. As it turned out, she was perhaps about three or four months old at the time we first met, yet she looked about 14 or 15 years old. When she was six months old, people would say, "Boy, how old is that dog? She looks like she's has been around for a long time!" When I would reply that she was six months old, inevitably there would be a long silence and sometimes the end of the conversation. She was never the kind of dog that would stimulate the beginning of a conversation on the beach with the guys I was hoping to meet, only with little old ladies who felt they had a kindred spirit in her.

Yet she was sweet, loving and very intelligent; exactly what I needed in a companion to help me erase the bitter memories of a broken love affair. She liked to sleep on my feet . . . no, not on the foot of the bed, but right on my feet. The solidity of her little round body would be felt every time I tried to turn over in the night. I felt as if my legs were under an anvil. We eventually made peace: she slept on my feet and I learned not to turn over in bed too often.

Suki was with me when I met my first husband. He was pleased that I had a dog, as he had a dog, too. His dog was not wanted in his home by his roommates because there was no longer any furniture to sit on. His dog had eaten it all. My friend was overjoyed because he thought if he left his dog with my dog, his dog would have something to do all day besides eat furniture. He did. His dog got my dog pregnant.

I had just returned home from a walk on the beach with Suki and although her looks hadn't improved to my eyes, to every male dog within a three mile radius, she was a temptress. She would elevate her tail and raise her head as if she was the Princess of the Dog Show. Male dogs came out of the woodwork and followed us down the strand, howling and moaning as if they were going to die. I soon figured it out . . . she must be in season. My friend's dog was only a baby of eight months, and so in my ignorance

I felt safe enough to leave them together long enough to call the animal hospital for an appointment for Suki to be "fixed."

When I turned around, Suki and my friend's dog were joined together in my living room! Oh, the horror of it. What could I do but sit there in astonishment and wait for something to happen? We all waited. They began to pant. Suki looked bored. His dog seemed tired. I called my friend on the phone and told him to come and get his sex fiend of a dog and take him away. We waited some more. I couldn't stand it and went outside to do some gardening. When my friend came after work for his dog, the two dogs were sitting on the living room carpet, napping. They looked so innocent, I figured maybe nothing happened and I had imagined it all.

Suki pregnant was a sight to behold. Her already round body became blimp-like as she squeezed carefully in and out of the doggie door. She no longer was able to walk or trot, but had adapted a sort of rolling, waddling gait to ease her swollen form from room to room. Thankfully, for the time being she gave up sleeping on my feet. She couldn't get up on the bed so I made a nest for her under the bed. I decided that she needed daily exercise to stay in shape, so I continued our afternoon walks on the beach. As soon as we would reach the sand, she would adapt her former strut and sway—up would come the tail and the head and she would sashay down the strand. The puppies inside went from side to side, in all likelihood becoming nauseated during their wild ride.

I had never attended a birth before I helped with Suki's. She alerted me at some wee hour of the morning by pulling the covers off the bed and trying to push them into her bed with her snout. Properly alerted and ready to attend to her every need, I sat by her nest as she pushed out her first baby. It seemed to be stuck inside of a sealed bag of some sort. Suki proceeded to eat the bag. I hoped that she knew what she was doing, as I sure didn't know. Lo and behold . . . it really was a puppy, slimy and icky. Suki licked the puppy clean and lay down again to sleep. I got back into bed.

Twenty minutes later, I awoke to find myself coverless again. Another puppy. This time I waited up with her and talked to my dog until the next puppy was on its way. We talked about things I had never discussed with a dog before. I poured out my heart to her, about the love I had lost and the emptiness I had inside of me until she had come along. She never complained . . . about my conversation or about the birth tremors she was experiencing. We stayed up all night, Suki and I . . . talking, giving birth and licking puppies . . . I involved in the first, she in the latter. She never cried or moaned once, just loved those little babies of hers from the moment they arrived. It was one of my most fulfilling life experiences.

None of the puppies looked like her or, for that matter, like my friend's dog, either. Of the six puppies, three looked like small black Labs and three looked like dachshunds with a black stripe down their backs. They were all cute. Friends of ours lined up for Suki's puppies and I never had to stand in front of the grocery store with a box.

My friend and I got married and moved. We took Suki and gave his dog away. I'm not sure he ever forgave me for that. We moved to an area that had open fields to run in and Suki took great advantage of that. She would run at full blast into the fields and disappear, except for integrated intervals when you could see the top of her head and her ears flapping high into the breeze. She would come out grinning and panting.

I'm not sure she ever caught a rabbit, but I know she gave it her best effort.

Suki would eat anything and all of it. One afternoon I made 250 chocolate chip cookies for a church meeting I was to attend that evening. Somehow Suki got into the bags of cookies and ate not some, not most, but *every single* cookie; all 250 of them. When I got home I wondered how she had become pregnant from one hour to the next. Only this time she was moaning, panting and definitely out of sorts. Not knowing what she had done, I rushed her to the animal hospital. The vet asked what had she eaten and I replied I hadn't fed her yet. His eyebrows disappeared into his hair. He said she *had* eaten, and a lot of it.

I left her there overnight and went home to find my contribution for the church dinner. Only where were the 250 cookies? I searched high and low. I was sure I had put them in the cupboard before I left home. I went into the backyard on a hunch and there, neatly stacked, were the nine plastic bags that earlier had contained the cookies. They weren't ripped or disheveled, only very empty. I called the vet and explained that 250 chocolate chip and oatmeal cookies were missing. He said impossible. *No* animal could eat 250 chocolate chip and oatmeal cookies and still be alive. He would watch her closely during the night. I never saw the cookies again, and Suki came home the next day. From that time on, she wasn't too fond of cookies but she would eat them if someone insisted.

There came the time when Suki's appearance and her age matched. She was 16 and having a difficult time getting around. Stairs had become too hard to climb and her kidneys were giving her fits. She had been my friend, at times my only loyal friend. Friendships with my human companions would vary and fade, but my friendship with Suki stayed steady and loyal through it all. I had divorced, remarried and was finally feeling as if my life was working. I couldn't stand to see her in such pain and so I decided to do the humane thing and put her to sleep for the last time.

I made an appointment and carried her in my arms to the car. She snuggled next to me as best she could despite the misery I knew she was feeling. She had never wanted me to worry about her; all she wanted from me was my love. In her whole life, she had never whined or cried. I did plenty for both of us. On the last drive together, I told her how much I loved her and how I was so proud of who she was. Her true beauty always had shone through and long ago I had forgotten how I once thought her to be ugly. I told her how I appreciated that she never begged for my attention and love, yet accepted it with the grace of one who knows they are deserving. If ever a royal animal had been born, it was she, for she had the ability to enjoy life with a dignity befitting a queen.

I carried her into the vet's office, and he asked me if I wanted to be with her in her last moments. I did. I held my arms around her while she lay on the cold, sterile table and tried to keep her warm when the vet went for the shot that was to end her life. She tried to get up, but she no longer could make her legs do what she wanted them to do. So for the longest time, we looked into each other's eyes ... liquid brown eyes, soft and trusting, into blue eyes overflowing with tears, as they are now. "Are you ready?" the vet asked. "I am," I answered. I lied. I would never in my life be ready to give up the love I had with Suki and I didn't want to give her up either. I knew I had to. I didn't want to break my connection with my Suki and I know she didn't want to either. Up until the last second, she looked into my eyes, and then I saw death creep into her gaze and I knew my best friend was gone.

I often think that if we human beings could duplicate the qualities that our animals exemplify to us, what a better world we would all live in. Suki showed me loyalty, love, understanding and compassion in an effortless way that was always ladylike and forgiving. If I could show my children the same unconditional love that Suki gave to me in the same consistent manner, I am sure my children would grow up to be the happiest and most secure individuals on the face of the planet. She set a good example for me and I will try to make her proud of me.

People say that when we die we are met on the other side by someone we know and love. I know who will be waiting for me . . . a little, round, black and white dog with an old face and a stubby tail that never stops wagging with joy at seeing her best friend again.

Patty Hansen

A Chaplain's Gift

When World War II was declared in 1939, I was seven years old; my brother was five. For the next four years we paid little attention to world affairs and felt childishly safe on our parents' farm, just west of the Alberta town of Rocky Mountain House. War bond drives and ration coupons only slightly affected our young lives. Even the enlistment of our two older brothers—one in the Army, the other in the Navy—meant little. We were much too young to understand the anxieties the adults experienced every time they read the newspapers or heard the nightly news broadcasts.

Neither of us heeded media reports of the devastation taking place on the various battlefields in Europe. However, the death of our older brother on an Italian battlefield and the events that occurred on our farm that day have made a lasting impression on both of us.

That winter day—December 7, 1943—began no differently than any other. My brother and I ate breakfast in silence while our mother listened to the 7 A.M. news on our old battery radio. "Today marks the second anniversary of the Japanese bombing of Pearl Harbor," the announcer reminded us. Then he went on to update the progress the Canadian Army was making. Tears filled Mother's eyes as she thought of her son, who was undoubtedly in the midst of it.

Angrily she exclaimed: "Leonard should have been sent home after he was wounded in Sicily. I hope he is strong enough to withstand the stress of combat so soon after being injured." Then, hoping to block out anything further that would intensify her fears, she reached up and turned off the radio.

We finished breakfast and completed last-minute preparations for school. After donning warm clothes we stepped outside, only to be greeted with a dreary day. There were ice crystals in the air and hoarfrost hung on the trees. Patches of fog drifted over the low-lying areas, making our one-and-a-half-mile walk unpleasant. School was even more depressing in the dimly lit one-room schoolhouse we attended. We were both relieved when the teacher dismissed us for the day.

We hurried home that afternoon, hunching our shoulders against the chill in the air. Along the way, we noticed our mother coming to meet us. That was unusual, and she explained: "I couldn't stay alone any longer. Something has happened that has upset me. After you left this morning, the dog began to howl. He has been howling all day." When she went out to water the horses at noon, she added, a white dove flew over her head. "I hope this is not a sign that something has happened to Leonard."

As we walked on, Mother continued to talk about my brother. She smiled a bit when she spoke of his love of music. Then she talked about his quiet ways, and the times he had been hurt because he had trusted the wrong people. "I have such an uneasy feeling about him."

Mother had been uneasy ever since Leonard's last leave before going overseas, when he had given away all his worldly possessions. I got the things he prized most—some pictures, his camera and a pair of leather chaps. He handed my mother his one good suit of clothes, instructing her to make it over for my younger brother. With tear-filled eyes he kissed us good-bye and said: "This is the last time you will see me. I'm not coming home."

By the time we got home we were all uneasy. The dog followed us to the house and continued to howl. We did the chores early, ate supper and settled down for the usual quiet evening, avoiding discussion of the day's events. Mother turned up the volume on the radio, hoping to muffle any unexpected noise. My brother and I dawdled over homework, trying to delay bedtime as long as possible. When we did retire we had trouble sleeping, for the memory of our mother's experience kept recurring.

After a restless night we rose the next morning to discover the fog had lifted, making the previous day's events seem less eerie. As the days wore on and no telegram arrived with bad news, Mother began to relax. When two weeks had gone by, she appeared convinced that the events of December 7 were just a coincidence. Soon Christmas was four days away. Our brother Russell was home on leave from the Navy, his last before sailing overseas. We had planned a party for him and invited friends to come for the day. After our father had left to pick them up, we hurried with dinner preparations. In our haste to make sure everything was just right, we failed to notice Father returning sooner than expected.

Father's face was ashen and tears filled his eyes. Everyone knew he had bad news. The telegram the local station agent had handed him just a short distance from our home was unopened. Mother took the envelope from his hand and tore it open. It read: *Regret deeply M102186 Private Walter Leonard Brierley officially killed in action 7th of December, 1943. Stop. Further information when received.*

Silence fell. Only Mother's quiet sobbing could be heard. My brother disappeared to his room; I hid behind the dining-room door so no one could see my tears. It was some time before Mother regained her composure. When she did, she told the rest of the family the puzzling events of that date. She sighed as she added, "I knew something terrible had happened. I believe God was preparing me for it."

On Christmas morning Mother was the first to rise. She lit the fire in the cookstove and prepared the bird for the oven. When breakfast was ready, the rest of us straggled to the table. Everyone tried to make the day special for Russell's sake, but we lacked enthusiasm. We opened our gifts quickly, trying not to think of the items so carefully chosen for Leonard's parcels.

Mother seemed to be in a trance as she prepared dinner. She made the usual generous portions—even though she knew little would be eaten. Knowing there would always be someone missing from her table in the future devastated her. Tears filled her eyes as she decorated the Christmas cake with tiny silver balls. Usually she had lots of help with the decorating, but that day she did it alone.

A subdued group gathered around the dining-room table for dinner. Everyone was trying to come to grips with what had happened. The usual non-stop exchange of noisy conversation gave way to periods of uncomfortable stillness. Father sat silent at the head of the table, no doubt remembering the many disagreements he and Leonard had had. My sister and older brothers recalled all the fun times they had had with Leonard. Then, with downcast eyes, they expressed regret for the times they had made his life uncomfortable. For the first time, everyone admitted that, when it came to a showdown, no one had ever gotten the better of Leonard. My younger brother ate quickly, pretending he was grown-up enough to understand why everyone was so quiet.

I sat beside Mother and picked at the food on my plate, tormented by what had happened. My mind raced with memories; the days my brother drove me to school in our old horse-drawn cutter, him waiting for me outside when classes were dismissed. Then I recalled warmer days when he had pulled me up behind him on his saddle horse. I remembered how Leonard had helped care for me when I became ill with scarlet fever and had to spend two months in bed. Then, when I developed rheumatic fever, he rode for the doctor and held me on his lap when the doctor sent me to the hospital.

Soon feelings of anger began crowding out my memories. I wanted to cry out and ask why we had wars, why Leonard had to die. But the words stuck in my throat like a foreign object. *It's not fair*, I thought. *Leonard was my hero. We shared secrets. We played Bluebird records on the gramophone and sang Wilf Carter songs together. He promised that one day he would teach me to yodel. Now it's too late. He's gone and we never said good-bye.*

My mother broke down and wept. "Poor Leonard. He always seemed so alone. He was too young to die. If only I could have been there to hold him and tell him one more time how much I loved him."

On Boxing Day we exchanged tearful good-byes with Russell as he boarded the bus to return to his ship. Unlike Leonard, he assured us the war would be over soon and he would be coming home unharmed.

Mother then began the double task of trying to come to grips with one son's death and another's leaving. Just when she was beginning to make progress, Leonard's letters written just days before his death arrived. They opened wounds just beginning to heal, but the assurance of his love for us and his wishes for a Merry Christmas made them a special bonus. The days that followed failed to lessen my mother's grief. She sewed a black ribbon on our coat sleeves and wore black when she went out. Neighbors came to visit. Friends wrote letters of sympathy and sent cards. The letters of condolence that arrived from the Department of National Defence, the prime minister and King George VI only seemed to deepen her sorrow. Then, one day, a letter arrived that brought a measure of peace.

The envelope bore the familiar "Passed by Censor" stamp and contained a neatly written letter from the chaplain of the Loyal Edmonton Regiment. Its contents assured her that her twenty-seven-year-old son had not died alone but was surrounded by caring, compassionate people. Dated December 12, 1943, it read:

Dear Mrs. Brierley,

It is with deep regret that I confirm the news of the death of your son, Pte. W. L. Brierley, M102186, who was killed in action on Dec. 7th, 1943, and was buried the same day. He was waiting to go over the top when a long-range shell burst near and he was mortally wounded in the abdomen. Nothing could have saved him although medical attention was near at hand, and he soon passed away. Pte. W. Barnett of the Edmontons was hit at the same time.

We buried him at a cemetery near (San) Leonardo with his comrades there to pay their last respects. It was a brief service conducted by myself as a unit chaplain. We were still under shell fire, but he was given a decent burial, and we put a cross at his head and some flowers for you.

He died so that others may live and peace come more quickly to a war-weary world. At the graveside we prayed that God might strengthen you in the days of your sorrow. All is well with him now, but you must

bear the burden of his passing as part of the world's
sacrifice for the evil that has been brought upon us.
   May God bless you until the day of reunion.
Yours sincerely,
Edgar J. Bailey, Chaplain

My mother read and reread that letter, each time
thanking God for the courage and compassion of the
chaplain who, under shell fire, was able to write such
words of comfort. After many months, Mother decided
to let go of the past. She placed the letter with my
brothers', tied them neatly, and stored them in her
cedar chest. But she never forgot the chaplain's words
or the events of December 7, 1943. She rarely spoke of
it, except to those close to her, but insisted until her
death in 1973 that what had happened on our farm
that day was no figment of her imagination.

My mother's grief was most evident on special
occasions: December 7, Christmas, my brother's
birthday, and especially Remembrance Day. Every
November 11 she took the Silver Cross from her jewelry box and pinned it on her lapel. Then, with heavy
heart, she joined other Silver Cross mothers at the
cenotaph to pay tribute to all who had given their
lives for their country.

I, too, continued to grieve. While walking to school
on cold winter days I would close my eyes and imagine Leonard was driving me. I longed to feel the
warmth of his body beneath our mother's old patch-
work quilt. And every time I rode horseback in the
rain, I felt dry and protected in his worn leather chaps.
I still miss him. Not a day goes by that I don't think
about him, about how handsome he was and how I
would have enjoyed having him around as I was
growing up. I think about how wonderful it would
have been for my children to have known their uncle.

In early 1991 I read a newspaper article about

chaplains at war. It contained interviews with three army chaplains, two of them then leaving for the Persian Gulf War. The third was Rev. Edgar Bailey, the World War II chaplain of the Loyal Eddies. After reading the article I contacted him and expressed as well as I could my thanks for the letter he had written my mother. The eighty-seven-year-old remembered my brother and related various events that had preceded his death. We talked and cried, then arranged to meet at the lodge in Edmonton where he now resided.

A month later, my husband and I visited the old gentleman. It was incredible! When we entered his room he immediately drew our attention to family pictures and war medals hanging on the wall. We chatted briefly about ourselves, then he handed us a scrapbook filled with notes and clippings covering nearly sixty years of his life. I could have spent the afternoon poring over its contents, but time was running short. Reluctantly, I put the scrapbook aside and started my tape recorder as he began to talk.

"Some people have asked what chaplains do in the war and why they are there. I think the best way to explain it is to tell you what General (Bernard) Montgomery said to me one time. He said, 'I would as soon go into battle without my artillery as without my chaplains.' Guns are of no use without the men behind them. The chaplains show the men that someone cares about them and is concerned about their loved ones back home."

When it was time for us to leave, he put his arms around me and kissed me tenderly on the cheek. His voice broke as he whispered, "That's from your brother." It was a time of sadness but also of joy. After forty-seven years I had finally been given an opportunity to properly say good-bye to Leonard. I thanked God for Edgar Bailey because He had provided that opportunity.

Dawn Philips

Remembering Ms. Murphy

Bored with the speed and hassles of highway driving, my husband and I decided to take "the road less traveled" to the beach last summer.

A stop in a small, nondescript town on Maryland's Eastern Shore led to an incident that will forever remain in our memory.

It began simply enough. A traffic light turned red. As we waited for the signal to change, I glanced at a faded brick nursing home.

Seated on a white wicker chair on the front porch was an elderly lady. Her eyes, intent upon mine, seemed to beckon, almost implore me to come to her.

The traffic light turned green. Suddenly I blurted, "Jim, park the car around the corner."

Taking Jim's hand, I headed toward the walkway to the nursing home. Jim stopped. "Wait a minute; we don't know anyone here." With gentle persuasion, I convinced my husband that my purpose was worthwhile.

The lady whose magnetic gaze had drawn me to her rose from her chair and, leaning on a cane, walked slowly toward us.

"I'm so glad you stopped," she smiled gratefully. "I prayed that you would. Have you a few minutes to sit and chat?" We followed her to a shady secluded spot on the side of the porch.

I was impressed by our hostess' natural beauty. She was slender, but not thin. Aside from the wrinkles at the corners of her hazel eyes, her ivory complexion was unlined, almost translucent. Her silky silver hair was tucked back neatly into a knot.

"Many people pass by here," she began, "especially in the summer. They peer from their car windows and see nothing more an old building that houses old people. But you saw me; Margaret Murphy. And you took time to stop." Thoughtfully, Margaret said, "Some people believe that all old people are senile; the truth is that we're just plain lonely." Then, self-mockingly she said, "But we old folks do rattle on, don't we?"

Fingering a beautiful diamond-framed oval cameo on the lace collar of her floral cotton dress, Margaret asked our names and where we were from. When I said, "Baltimore," her face brightened and her eyes sparkled. She said, "My sister, bless her soul, lived on Gorusch Avenue in Baltimore all her life."

Excitedly I explained, "As a child, I lived just a few blocks away on Homestead Street. What was your sister's name?" Immediately, I remembered Marie Gibbons. She had been my classmate and best girl-friend. For over an hour, Margaret and I shared reminiscences of our youth.

We were engaged in animated conversation when a nurse appeared with a glass of water and two small pink tablets. "I'm sorry to interrupt," she said pleasantly, "but it's time for your medication and afternoon nap, Miss Margaret. We've got to keep that ticker ticking, you know," she said, smiling and handing Margaret the medicine. Jim and I exchanged glances.

Without protest, Margaret swallowed the pills. "Can't I stay with my friends a few minutes longer, Miss Baxter?" Margaret asked. Kindly but firmly, the nurse refused.

Miss Baxter extended her arm and helped Margaret from the chair. We assured her that we would stop and see her the following week when we returned from the beach. Her unhappy expression changed to gladness. "That would be wonderful," Margaret said.

After a sunny week, the day Jim and I left for home was cloudy and damp. The nursing home seemed especially dreary under the slate-colored clouds.

After we waited a few minutes, Miss Baxter appeared. She handed us a small box with a letter attached. Then she held my hand as Jim read the letter:

Dear Ones,

These past few days have been the happiest ones in my life since Henry, my beloved husband, died two years ago. Once more, I have a family I love and who cares about me.

Last night the doctor seemed concerned about my heart problem. However, I feel wonderful. And while I'm in this happy mood, I want to thank you for the joy you both have brought into my life.

Beverly dear, this gift for you is the cameo brooch I wore the day we met. My husband gave it to me on our wedding day, June 30, 1939. It had belonged to his mother. Enjoy wearing it, and hope that someday it will belong to your daughters and their children. With the brooch comes my everlasting love.

Margaret

Three days after our visit, Margaret died peacefully in her sleep. Teardrops stained my cheeks as I held the cameo in my hands. Tenderly, I turned it over and read the inscription engraved on the sterling silver rim of the brooch: "Love is forever."

So are memories, dear Margaret, so are memories.

Beverly Fine

A Young Girl Still Dwells

The following poem was written by a woman who
worked as a nurse in the old folks' ward of Sunnyside
Royal Hospital in Montrose, Scotland. It first
appeared as an anonymous submission in the hospital's staff magazine. Several months later, the staff of
Ashludie Hospital near Dundee, Scotland, found a
hand-written copy of the poem among the possessions of an elderly patient who had recently died. The
poem so impressed the staff that copies were widely
distributed throughout the hospital and beyond. The
poem's original author was eventually discovered.
She died, at age 80, in her sleep.

What do you see, nurse, what do you see?
Are you thinking when you look at me—
A crabbed old woman, not very wise,
Uncertain of habit with faraway eyes?
Who dribbles her food and makes no reply
When you say in a loud voice, "I do wish you'd try!"
Who seems not to notice the things that you do,
And forever is losing a stocking or shoe?
Who resisting or not, lets you do as you will
With bathing and feeding, the long day to fill?
Is that what you're thinking, is that what you see?
Then open your eyes, nurse, you're looking at me.

I'll tell you who I am as I sit here so still.
As I move at your bidding, eat at your will . . .
I'm a small child of ten with a father and mother,
Brothers and sisters who love one another;
A young girl of sixteen with wings on her feet,
Dreaming that soon a love she'll meet;
A bride at twenty my heart gives a leap,
Remembering the vows that I promised to keep;
At twenty-five now I have young of my own
Who need me to build a secure, happy home;
A woman of thirty, my young now grow fast,
Bound together with ties that should last;
At forty, my young sons have grown up and gone,
But my man's beside me to see I don't mourn;
At fifty, once more babies play round my knee,
Again we know children my loved ones and me.
Dark days are upon me; my husband is dead,
I look at the future, I shudder with dread.
For my young are all rearing young of their own,
And I think of the years and the love that I've known.
I'm an old woman now and nature is cruel;
'Tis her jest to make old age look like a fool.
The body it crumbles, grace and vigor depart;
There is a stone where I once had a heart.
But inside this old carcass a young girl still dwells,
And now, again, my embittered heart swells.
I remember the joys, I remember the pain,
And I'm loving and living life over again,
I think of the years, all too few, gone too fast,
And accept the stark fact that nothing can last.
So open your eyes, nurse, open and see
Not a crabbed old woman,
Look closer—see me!

Phyllis McCormack
Submitted by Ronald Dahlsten

Reprinted by permission of Michael McCormack. © Michael McCormack.

A Final Goodbye

"I am going home to Denmark, Son, and I just wanted to tell you I love you."

In my dad's last telephone call to me, he repeated that line seven times in a half hour. I wasn't listening at the right level. I heard the words, but not the message, and certainly not their profound intent. I believed my dad would live to be over 100 years old, as my great-uncle lived to be 107 years old. I had not felt his remorse over Mom's death, understood his intense loneliness as an "empty nester," or realized most of his pals had long since light-beamed off the planet. He relentlessly requested my brothers and I create grand-children so that he could be a devoted grandfather. I was too busy "entrepreneuring" to really listen.

"Dad's dead," sighed my brother Brian on July 4, 1982.

My little brother is a witty lawyer and has a humor-ous, quick mind. I thought he was setting me up for a joke, and I awaited the punchline—there wasn't one. "Dad died in the bed he was born in—in Rozkeldj," continued Brian. "The funeral directors are putting him in a coffin, and shipping Dad and his belongings to us by tomorrow. We need to prepare for the funeral."

I was speechless. This isn't the way it's supposed to happen. If I knew these were to be Dad's final days, I would have asked to go with him to Denmark. I believe in the hospice movement, which says: "No one should die alone." A loved one should hold your hand and comfort you as you transition from one plane of reality to another. I would have offered consolation during his final hour, if I'd been really listening, thinking and in tune with the Infinite. Dad announced his departure as best he could, and I had missed it. I felt grief, pain and remorse. Why had I not been there for him? He'd always been there for me.

In the mornings when I was nine years old, he would come home from working 18 hours at his bakery and wake me up at 5:00 A.M. by scratching my back with his strong, powerful hands and whispering, "Time to get up, Son." By the time I was dressed and ready to roll, he had my newspapers folded, banded and stuffed in my bicycle basket. Recalling his generosity of spirit brings tears to my eyes.

When I was racing bicycles, he drove me 50 miles each way to Kenosha, Wisconsin, every Tuesday night so I could race and he could watch me. He was there to hold me if I lost and shared the euphoria when I won.

Later, he accompanied me to all my local talks in Chicago when I spoke to Century 21, Mary Kay, Equitable and various churches. He always smiled, listened and proudly told whomever he was sitting with, "That's my boy!"

After the fact, my heart was in pain because Dad was there for me and I wasn't there for him. My humble advice is to always, always share your love with your loved ones, and ask to be invited to that sacred transitional period where physical life transforms into spiritual life. Experiencing the process of death with one you love will take you into a bigger, more expansive dimension of beingness.

Mark Victor Hansen

Do It Today!

If you were going to die soon and had only one phone call you could make, who would you call and what would you say? And why are you waiting?

Stephen Levine

When I was superintendent of schools in Palo Alto, California, Polly Tyner, the president of our board of trustees, wrote a letter that was printed in the *Palo Alto Times*. Polly's son, Jim, had great difficulty in school. He was classified as educationally handicapped and required a great deal of patience on the part of his parents and teachers. But Jim was a happy kid with a great smile that lit up the room. His parents acknowledged his academic difficulties, but always tried to help him see his strengths so that he could walk with pride. Shortly after Jim finished high school, he was killed in a motorcycle accident. After his death, his mother submitted this letter to the newspaper.

> *Today we buried our 20-year-old son. He was killed instantly in a motorcycle accident on Friday night. How I wish I had known when I talked to him last that it would be the last time. If I had only*

known I would have said, "Jim, I love you and I'm so very proud of you."

I would have taken the time to count the many blessings he brought to the lives of the many who loved him. I would have taken time to appreciate his beautiful smile, the sound of his laughter, his genuine love of people.

When you put all the good attributes on the scale and you try to balance all the irritating traits such as the radio which was always too loud, the haircut that wasn't to our liking, the dirty socks under the bed, etc., the irritations don't amount to much.

I won't get another chance to tell my son all I would have wanted him to hear, but, other parents, you do have a chance. Tell your young people what you would want them to hear if you knew it would be your last conversation. The last time I talked to Jim was the day he died. He called me to say, "Hi, Mom! I just called to say I love you. Got to go to work. Bye." He gave me something to treasure forever.

If there is any purpose at all to Jim's death, maybe it is to make others appreciate more of life and to have people, especially families, take the time to let each other know just how much we care.

You may never have another chance. Do it today!

Robert Reasoner

An Act of Kindness for a Broken Heart

*I am only one. But still, I am one. I cannot
do everything, but still I can do something.
And because I cannot do everything, I will
not refuse to do the something that I can do.*
Edward Everett Hale

My husband, Hanoch, and I wrote a book, *Acts of Kindness: How to Create a Kindness Revolution*, which has generated much interest across America. This story was shared with us by an anonymous caller during a radio talk show in Chicago.

"Hi, Mommy, what are you doing?" asked Susie.

"I'm making a casserole for Mrs. Smith next door," said her mother.

"Why?" asked Susie, who was only six years old.

"Because Mrs. Smith is very sad; she lost her daughter and she has a broken heart. We need to take care of her for a little while."

"Why, Mommy?"

"You see, Susie, when someone is very, very sad, they have trouble doing the little things like making dinner or other chores. Because we're part of a community and Mrs. Smith is our neighbor, we need to do some things to help her. Mrs. Smith won't ever be able to talk with her daughter or hug her or do all those wonderful things that mommies and daughters do together. You are a very smart girl, Susie; maybe you'll think of some way to help take care of Mrs. Smith."

Susie thought seriously about this challenge and how she could do her part in caring for Mrs. Smith. A few minutes later, Susie knocked on her door. After a few moments Mrs. Smith answered the knock with a "Hi, Susie."

Susie noticed that Mrs. Smith didn't have that familiar musical quality about her voice when she greeted someone.

Mrs. Smith also looked as though she might have been crying because her eyes were watery and swollen.

"What can I do for you, Susie?" asked Mrs. Smith.

"My mommy says that you lost your daughter and you're very, very sad with a broken heart." Susie held her hand out shyly. In it was a Band-Aid. "This is for your broken heart." Mrs. Smith gasped, choking back her tears. She knelt down and hugged Susie. Through her tears she said, "Thank you, darling girl, this will help a lot."

Mrs. Smith accepted Susie's act of kindness and took it one step further. She purchased a small key ring with a plexiglass picture frame—the ones designed to carry keys and proudly display a family portrait at the same time. Mrs. Smith placed Susie's Band-Aid in the frame to remind herself to heal a little every time she sees it. She wisely knows that healing takes time and support. It has become her symbol for healing, while not forgetting the joy and love she experienced with her daughter.

Meladee McCarty

See You in the Morning

Because of my mother and her wisdom I have no fear of death. She was my best friend and my greatest teacher. Every time we parted company, whether it was to retire for the evening or before one of us was about to depart on a trip, she would say, "I'll see you in the morning." It was a promise she always kept.

My grandfather was a minister and in those days, around the turn of the century, whenever a member of the congregation passed on, the body would lie in state in the minister's parlor. To an eight-year-old girl, this can be a most frightening experience.

One day, my grandfather picked up my mother, carried her into the parlor and asked her to feel the wall.

"What does that feel like, Bobbie?" he asked.

"Well, it's hard and it's cold," she replied.

Then he carried her over to the casket and said, "Bobbie, I'm going to ask you to do the most difficult thing I'll ever ask. But if you do it, you'll never be afraid of death again. I want you to put your hand on Mr. Smith's face."

Because she loved and trusted him so much she was able to fulfill his request. "Well?" asked my grandfather. "Daddy," she said, "it feels like the wall."

"That's right," he said. "This is his old house and our friend, Mr. Smith, has moved and Bobbie, there's no reason to be afraid of an old house."

The lesson took root and grew the rest of her life. She had absolutely no fear of death. Eight hours before she left us, she made a most unusual request. As we stood around her bed fighting back tears, she said, "Don't bring any flowers to my grave because I won't be there. When I get rid of this body, I'm flying to Europe. Your father would never take me." The room erupted in laughter and there were no more tears the rest of the night.

As we kissed her and bade her goodnight, she smiled and said, "I'll see you in the morning."

However, at 6:15 A.M. the next day, I received the call from the doctor that she had begun her flight to Europe.

Two days later, we were in my parents' apartment going through my mother's things when we came across a huge file of her writings. As I opened the packet, one piece of paper fell to the floor.

It was the following poem. I don't know if it was one she had written or someone else's work that she had lovingly saved. All I know is that it was the only piece of paper to fall and it read:

The Legacy

When I die, give what is left of me to children.
If you need to cry, cry for your brothers walking
*   beside you.*
Put your arms around anyone and give them what
*   you need to give to me.*
I want to leave you with something, something
*   better than words or sounds.*
Look for me in the people I have known and loved.

And if you cannot live without me, then let me
   live on in your eyes, your mind and your acts
   of kindness.
You can love me most by letting hands touch
   hands and letting go of children that need to be
   free.
Love does not die, people do.
So when all that is left of me is love . . .
Give me away . . .

My dad and I smiled at each other as we felt her presence, and it was morning once again.

John Wayne Schlatter

Love Never Leaves You

I grew up in a very normal family with two brothers and two sisters. Although we did not have much money in those days, I always remember my mother and father taking us out for weekend picnics or to the zoo.

My mother was a very loving and caring person. She was always ready to help someone else and she often brought home stray or injured animals. Even though she had five children to contend with, she always found time to help others.

I think back to my early childhood and I see my parents not as husband and wife with five children, but as a newlywed couple very much in love. The daytime was to be spent with us kids, but the night was their time to be with each other.

I remember I was lying in bed one night. It was Sunday, May 27, 1973. I woke up to the sound of my parents coming home from a night out with some friends. They were laughing and playing around and when I heard them go to bed, I rolled over and went back to sleep, but all that night my sleep was troubled by nightmares.

Monday morning, May 28, 1973, I awoke to a cloudy overcast day. My mother was not up yet so we all got ourselves ready and went to school. All that day, I had this very empty feeling inside. I came home after school and let myself into the house. "Hi, Ma, I'm home." No answer. The house seemed very cold and empty. I was afraid. Trembling, I climbed the stairs and went to my parents' room. The door was only open a little and I could not see all the way inside. "Ma?" I pushed the door open all the way so I could see the whole room, and there was my mother lying on the floor beside the bed. I tried to wake her, but she would not wake up. I knew she was dead. I turned around, left the room and went downstairs. I sat on the couch in silence for a very long time until my older sister came home. She saw me sitting there and then in a flash she was running up the stairs.

I sat in the living room and watched as my father talked to the policeman. I watched the ambulance attendants carry out the stretcher with my mother on it. All I could do was sit and watch. I couldn't even cry. I had never thought of my father as an old man, but when I saw him that day he never looked so old as he did then.

Tuesday, May 29, 1973. My 11th birthday. There was no singing, no party or cake, just silence as we sat around the dining room table looking at our food. It was my fault. If I had come home sooner she would still be alive. If I had been older she would still be alive. If . . .

For many years, I carried around the guilt of my mother's death. I thought about all the things I should have done. All the nasty things I had said to her. I truly believed that because I was a troublesome child, God was punishing me by taking away my mother. The thing that troubled me the most was the fact I never got the chance to say goodbye. I would never again feel her warm embrace, smell the sweet scent of her perfume or feel her gentle kisses as she tucked me into my bed at night. All these things taken away from me were my punishment.

May 29, 1989: my 27th birthday, and I was feeling very lonely and empty. I had never recovered from the effects of my mother's death. I was an emotional mess. My anger at God had hit its peak. I was crying and screaming at God. "Why did you take her away from me? You never even gave me the chance to say goodbye. I loved her and you took that away from me. I only wanted to hold her one more time. *I hate you!*" I sat in my living room sobbing. I felt drained when suddenly a warm feeling came over me. I could physically feel two arms embrace me. I could sense a familiar but long-forgotten fragrance in the room. It was her. I could feel her presence. I felt her touch and smelled her fragrance. The God that I had hated had granted me my wish. My mother was coming to me when I needed her.

I know today my mother is always with me. I still love her with all my heart, and I know that she will always be there for me. Just when I had given up and resigned myself to the fact that she was gone forever, she let me know that her love would never leave me.

Stanley D. Moulson

The Prettiest Angel

The heart of a fool is in his mouth, but the mouth of a wise man is in his heart.
Benjamin Franklin

For the past 20 years I have spoken to all kinds of audiences in the character of Benjamin Franklin. Even though the majority of my engagements are before corporate and convention audiences, I still like to talk to school groups. When I work for corporate clients outside the Philadelphia area, I ask them to sponsor appearances in two schools as a service to their community.

I find that even very young children relate well to the message I present through the character of Benjamin Franklin. I always encourage them to ask any questions they wish, so I usually get some interesting ones. The character of Benjamin Franklin often becomes so real to these students that they willingly suspend disbelief and are caught up in a dialogue with me as if I am really Ben Franklin.

On one particular day after an assembly for an elementary school, I was visiting a fifth-grade classroom to answer questions for students who were studying American history. One student raised his hand and said, "I thought you died." This was not an unusual question and I answered it by saying, "Well, I did die on April 17, 1790, when I was 84 years old, but I didn't like it and I'm never going to do it again."

I immediately asked for any other questions and called on a boy at the back of the room who raised his hand. He asked, "When you were in Heaven, did you see my mother there?"

My heart stopped. I wanted the floor to open up and swallow me. My only thought was, "Don't blow this!" I realized for an 11-year-old boy to ask that question in front of all of his classmates it had to either be a very recent occurrence or of utmost concern. I also knew I had to say something.

Then I heard my voice say: "I'm not sure if she is the one I think she was, but if she is, she was the prettiest angel there."

The smile on his face told me that it was the right answer. I'm not sure where it came from, but I think I just may have had a little help from the prettiest angel there.

Ralph Archbold

4
A
MATTER
OF
ATTITUDE

The greatest discovery of my generation is that human beings can alter their lives by altering their attitudes of mind.

William James

Discouraged?

As I was driving home from work one day, I stopped to watch a local Little League baseball game that was being played in a park near my home. As I sat down behind the bench on the first-baseline, I asked one of the boys what the score was.

"We're behind 14 to nothing," he answered with a smile.

"Really," I said. "I have to say you don't look very discouraged."

"Discouraged?" the boy asked with a puzzled look on his face. "Why should we be discouraged? We haven't been up to bat yet."

Jack Canfield

A Place to Stand

Those who wish to sing always find a song.
Swedish proverb

Most people are about as happy as they make up their minds to be.
Abraham Lincoln

If you have ever gone through a toll booth, you know that your relationship to the person in the booth is not the most intimate you'll ever have. It is one of life's frequent nonencounters: You hand over some money; you might get change; you drive off. I have been through every one of the 17 toll booths on the Oakland-San Francisco Bay Bridge on thousands of occasions, and never had an exchange worth remembering with anybody.

Late one morning in 1984, headed for lunch in San Francisco, I drove toward one of the booths. I heard loud music. It sounded like a party, or a Michael Jackson concert. I looked around. No other cars with their windows open. No sound trucks. I looked at the toll booth. Inside it, the man was dancing.

"What are you doing?" I asked.

"I'm having a party," he said.

"What about the rest of these people?" I looked over at other booths; nothing moving there.

"They're not invited."

I had a dozen other questions for him, but somebody in a big hurry to get somewhere started punching his horn behind me and I drove off. But I made a note to myself: Find this guy again. There's something in his eye that says there's magic in his toll booth.

Months later I did find him again, still with the loud music, still having a party.

Again I asked, "What are you doing?"

He said, "I remember you from the last time. I'm still dancing. I'm having the same party."

I said, "Look. What about the rest of the people . . ."

He said. "Stop. What do those look like to you?" He pointed down the row of toll booths.

"They look like . . . toll booths."

"Nooooo imagination!"

I said, "Okay, I give up. What do they look like to you?"

He said, "Vertical coffins."

"What are you talking about?"

"I can prove it. At 8:30 every morning, live people get in. Then they die for eight hours. At 4:30, like Lazarus from the dead, they reemerge and go home. For eight hours, brain is on hold, dead on the job. Going through the motions."

I was amazed. This guy had developed a philosophy, a mythology about his job. I could not help asking the next question: "Why is it different for you? You're having a good time."

He looked at me. "I knew you were going to ask that," he said. "I'm going to be a dancer someday." He pointed to the administration building. "My bosses are in there, and they're paying for my training."

Sixteen people dead on the job, and the seventeenth, in precisely the same situation, figures out a way to *live*. That man was having a party where you and I would probably not last three days. The boredom! He and I did have lunch later, and he said, "I don't understand why anybody would think my job is boring. I have a corner office, glass on all sides. I can see the Golden Gate, San Francisco, the Berkeley hills; half the Western world vacations here . . . and I just stroll in every day and practice dancing."

Dr. Charles Garfield

The Window

And life is what we make it, always has
been, always will be.

Grandma Moses

There were once two men, both seriously ill, in the same small room of a great hospital. Quite a small room, it had one window looking out on the world. One of the men, as part of his treatment, was allowed to sit up in bed for an hour in the afternoon (something to do with draining the fluid from his lungs). His bed was next to the window. But the other man had to spend all his time flat on his back.

Every afternoon when the man next to the window was propped up for his hour, he would pass the time by describing what he could see outside. The window apparently overlooked a park where there was a lake. There were ducks and swans in the lake, and children came to throw them bread and sail model boats. Young lovers walked hand in hand beneath the trees, and there were flowers and stretches of grass, games of softball. And at the back, behind the fringe of trees, was a fine view of the city skyline.

The man on his back would listen to the other man describe all of this, enjoying every minute. He heard how a child nearly fell into the lake, and how beautiful the girls were in their summer dresses. His friend's descriptions eventually made him feel he could almost see what was happening outside.

Then one fine afternoon, the thought struck him: Why should the man next to the window have all the pleasure of seeing what was going on? Why shouldn't he get the chance? He felt ashamed, but the more he tried not to think like that, the worse he wanted a change. He'd do anything! One night as he stared at the ceiling, the other man suddenly woke up, coughing and choking, his hands groping for the button that would bring the nurse running. But the man watched without moving—even when the sound of breathing stopped. In the morning, the nurse found the other man dead, and quietly took his body away.

As soon as it seemed decent, the man asked if he could be switched to the bed next to the window. So they moved him, tucked him in, and made him quite comfortable. The minute they left, he propped himself up on one elbow, painfully and laboriously, and looked out the window.

It faced a blank wall.

George Target
Submitted by Ronald Dahlsten and Harriette Lindsey

The Optimist

There is a story of identical twins. One was a hope-filled optimist. "Everything is coming up roses!" he would say. The other was a sad and hopeless pessimist. He thought that Murphy, as in Murphy's Law, was an optimist. The worried parents of the boys brought them to the local psychologist.

He suggested to the parents a plan to balance the twins' personalities. "On their next birthday, put them in separate rooms to open their gifts. Give the pessimist the best toys you can afford, and give the optimist a box of manure." The parents followed these instructions and carefully observed the results.

When they peeked in on the pessimist, they heard him audibly complaining, "I don't like the color of this computer. . . . I'll bet this calculator will break. . . . I don't like this game. . . . I know someone who's got a bigger toy car than this. . . ."

Tiptoeing across the corridor, the parents peeked in and saw their little optimist gleefully throwing the manure up in the air. He was giggling. "You can't fool me! Where there's this much manure, there's gotta be a pony!"

Author Unknown
from More Sower's Seeds *by Brian Cavanaugh*

Millie's Mother's Red Dress

It hung there in the closet
While she was dying, Mother's red dress,
Like a gash in the row
Of dark, old clothes
She had worn away her life in.

They had called me home
And I knew when I saw her
She wasn't going to last.

When I saw the dress, I said
"Why, Mother—how beautiful!
I've never seen it on you."

"I've never worn it," she slowly said.
"Sit down, Millie—I'd like to undo
A lesson or two before I go, if I can."

I sat by her bed
And she sighed a bigger breath
Than I thought she could hold.
"Now that I'll soon be gone,
I can see some things.
Oh, I taught you good—but I taught you wrong."

"What do you mean, Mother?"
"Well—I always thought
That a good woman never takes her turn,
That she's just for doing for somebody else.
Do here, do there, always keep
Everybody else's wants tended and make sure
Yours are at the bottom of the heap.

"Maybe someday you'll get to them.
But of course you never do.
My life was like that—doing for your dad,
Doing for the boys, for your sisters, for you."

"You did—everything a mother could."

"Oh, Millie, Millie, it was no good—
For you—for him. Don't you see?
I did you the worst of wrongs.
I asked for nothing—for me!

"Your father in the other room,
All stirred up and staring at the walls—
When the doctor told him, he took
It bad—came to my bed and all but shook
The life right out of me. 'You can't die,
Do you hear? What'll become of me?'
"'What'll become of me?'
It'll be hard, all right, when I go.
He can't even find the frying pan, you know.

"And you children—
I was a free ride for everybody, everywhere.
I was the first one up and the last one down
Seven days out of the week.
I always took the toast that got burned.
And the very smallest piece of pie.

"I look at how some of your brothers
Treat their wives now
And it makes me sick, 'cause it was me
That taught it to them. And they learned.
They learned that a woman doesn't
Even exist except to give.
Why, every single penny that I could save
Went for your clothes, or your books,
Even when it wasn't necessary.
Can't even remember once when I took
Myself downtown to buy something beautiful—
For me.

"Except last year when I got that red dress.
I found I had twenty dollars
That wasn't especially spoke for.
I was on my way to pay it extra on the washer.
But somehow—I came home with this big box.
Your father really gave it to me then.
'Where you going to wear a thing like that to—
Some opera or something?'
And he was right, I guess.
I've never, except in the store,
Put on that dress.

"Oh Millie—I always thought if you take
Nothing for yourself in this world
You'd have it all in the next somehow
I don't believe that anymore.
I think the Lord wants us to have something—
Here—and now.

"And I'm telling you, Millie, if some miracle
Could get me off this bed, you could look
For a different mother, 'cause I would be one.
Oh, I passed up my turn so long

I would hardly know how to take it.
But I'd learn, Millie.
I would learn!"

It hung there in the closet
While she was dying, Mother's red dress,
Like a gash in the row
Of dark, old clothes
She had worn away her life in.

Her last words to me were these:
"Do me the honor, Millie,
Of not following in my footsteps.
Promise me that."

I promised.
She caught her breath
Then Mother took her turn
In death.

                    Carol Lynn Pearson

Used by Permission of Carol Lynn Pearson, 1976

Attitude—One of Life's Choices

A happy person is not a person in a certain set of circumstances, but rather a person with a certain set of attitudes.

Hugh Downs

My wife, Tere, and I purchased a new car in December. Even though we had tickets to fly from California to Houston to visit her family for Christmas, we decided to drive to Texas to break in the new car. We packed the car and took off for a wonderful week with Grandma.

We had a wonderful time and stayed to the last possible minute visiting with Grandma. On the return trip we needed to get home in a hurry, so we drove straight through—one person driving while the other one slept. After driving in a hard rain for several hours, we arrived home late at night. We were tired and ready for a hot shower and a soft bed. I had the feeling that no matter how tired we were, we should unpack the car that night, but all Tere wanted was the hot shower and the soft bed, so we decided to wait and unload the car in the morning.

At seven o'clock in the morning, we got up refreshed and ready to unpack the car. When we opened the front door, there was no car in the driveway! Tere and I looked at each other, looked back at the driveway, looked at each other, looked back at the driveway, and looked at each other again. Then Tere asked this wonderful question, "Well, where did you park the car?"

Laughing, I answered, "Right in the driveway." Now we knew where we had parked the car, but we still walked outside, hoping that maybe the car had miraculously backed out the driveway and parked itself by the curb, but it hadn't.

Stunned, we called the police and filed a report that supposedly activated our high-tech tracking system. To be on the safe side, I also called the tracking system company. They assured me they had a 98 percent recovery rate within two hours. In two hours, I called again and asked, "Where's my car?"

"We haven't found it yet, Mr. Harris, but we have a 94 percent recovery rate within four hours."

Two more hours passed. I called again and asked, "Where's my car?"

Again they answered, "We haven't found it yet, but we have a 90 percent recovery rate of finding it within eight hours."

At that point I told them, "Your percentage rate means nothing to me when I'm in the small percentage, so call me when you find it."

Later that day, a commercial aired on television with the automaker asking, "Wouldn't you like to have this car in your driveway?"

I responded, "Sure I would! I had one yesterday."

As the day unfolded, Tere became increasingly upset as she remembered more and more of what had been in the car—our wedding album, irreplaceable family photos from past generations, clothes, all of our camera equipment, my wallet and our checkbooks, just to name a few. These were items of little importance to our survival, yet they seemed of major importance at that moment.

Anxious and frustrated, Tere asked me, "How can you joke about this when all of these things and our brand new car are missing?"

I looked at her and said, "Honey, we can have a stolen car and be all upset, or we can have a stolen car and be happy. Either way, we have a stolen car. I truly believe our attitudes and moods are our choice and right now I choose to be happy."

Five days later our car was returned without a trace of any of our belongings, and with over $3,000 worth of damage to the car. I took it to the dealer for repair and was happy to hear they would have it back to us within a week.

At the end of that week, I dropped off the rental and picked up our car. I was excited and relieved to have our own car back. Unfortunately, these feelings were short-lived. On the way home, I rear-ended another car right at our freeway exit ramp. It didn't hurt the car I ran into, but it sure hurt ours—another $3,000 worth of damage and another insurance claim. I managed to drive the car into our driveway, but when I got out to survey the damage, the left front tire went flat.

As I was standing in the driveway looking at the car, kicking myself in the tail for hitting the other car, Tere arrived home. She walked up to me, looked at the car, and then at me. Seeing I was beating myself up, she put her arm around me and said, "Honey, we can have a wrecked car and be all upset, or we can have a wrecked car and be happy. Either way, we have a wrecked car, so let's choose to be happy."

I surrendered with a hearty laugh and we went on to have a wonderful evening together.

Bob Harris

5

ON LEARNING AND TEACHING

One hundred years from now it will not matter what kind of car you drove, what kind of house you lived in, how much you had in your bank account, or what your clothes looked like. But the world may be a little better because you were important in the life of a child.

Margaret Fishback Powers

Copyright ©1995 by Margaret Fishback Powers.

"Mrs. Hammond! I'd know you anywhere
from little Billy's Portrait of you."

Drawing by Frascino; ©1988
The New Yorker Magazine, Inc.

The Magic Pebbles

It is the habitual thought that frames itself into our life. It affects us even more than our intimate social relations do. Our confidential friends have not so much to do in shaping our lives as the thoughts which we harbor.

J.W. Teal

"Why do we have to learn all of this dumb stuff?" Of all the complaints and questions I have heard from my students during my years in the classroom, this was the one most frequently uttered. I would answer it by recounting the following legend.

> One night a group of nomads were preparing to retire for the evening when suddenly they were surrounded by a great light. They knew they were in the presence of a celestial being. With great anticipation, they awaited a heavenly message of great importance that they knew must be especially for them.
>
> Finally, the voice spoke. "Gather as many pebbles as you can. Put them in your saddle bags. Travel a day's journey and tomorrow night will find you glad and it will find you sad."

After having departed, the nomads shared their disappointment and anger with each other. They had expected the revelation of a great universal truth that would enable them to create wealth, health and purpose for the world. But instead they were given a menial task that made no sense to them at all. However, the memory of the brilliance of their visitor caused each one to pick up a few pebbles and deposit them in their saddle bags while voicing their displeasure.

They traveled a day's journey and that night while making camp, they reached into their saddle bags and discovered every pebble they had gathered had become a diamond. They were glad they had diamonds. They were sad they had not gathered more pebbles.

It was an experience I had with a student, I shall call Alan, early in my teaching career that illustrated the truth of that legend to me.

When Alan was in the eighth grade, he majored in "trouble" with a minor in "suspensions." He had studied how to be a bully and was getting his master's in "thievery."

Every day I had my students memorize a quotation from a great thinker. As I called roll, I would begin a quotation. To be counted present, the student would be expected to finish the thought.

"Alice Adams— 'There is no failure except . . .'"

"'In no longer trying.' I'm present, Mr. Schlatter."

So, by the end of the year, my young charges would have memorized 150 great thoughts.

"Think you can, think you can't—either way you're right!"

"If you can see the obstacles, you've taken your eyes off the goal."

"A cynic is someone who knows the price of everything and the value of nothing."

And, of course, Napoleon Hill's "If you can conceive it, and believe it, you can achieve it."

No one complained about this daily routine more than Alan—right up to the day he was expelled and I lost touch with him for five years. Then one day, he called. He was in a special program at one of the neighboring colleges and had just finished parole.

He told me that after being sent to juvenile hall and finally being shipped off to the California Youth Authority for his antics, he had become so disgusted with himself that he had taken a razor blade and cut his wrists.

He said, "You know what, Mr. Schlatter, as I lay there with my life running out of my body, I suddenly remembered that dumb quote you made me write 20 times one day. 'There is no failure except in no longer trying.' Then it suddenly made sense to me. As long as I was alive, I wasn't a failure, but if I allowed myself to die, I would most certainly die a failure. So with my remaining strength, I called for help and started a new life."

At the time he had heard the quotation, it was a pebble. When he needed guidance in a moment of crisis, it had become a diamond. And so it is to you I say, gather all the pebbles you can, and you can count on a future filled with diamonds.

John Wayne Schlatter

We're the Retards

On my first day of teaching, all my classes were going well. Being a teacher was going to be a cinch, I decided. Then came period seven, the last class of the day.

As I walked toward the room, I heard furniture crash. Rounding the corner, I saw one boy pinning another to the floor. "Listen, you retard!" yelled the one on the bottom. "I don't give a damn about your sister!"

"You keep your hands off her, you hear me?" the boy on top threatened.

I drew up my short frame and asked them to stop fighting. Suddenly, 14 pairs of eyes were riveted on my face. I knew I did not look convincing. Glaring at each other and me, the two boys slowly took their seats. At that moment, the teacher from across the hall stuck his head in the door and shouted at my students to sit down, shut up and do what I said. I was left feeling powerless.

I tried to teach the lesson I had prepared but was met with a sea of guarded faces. As the class was leaving, I detained the boy who had instigated the fight. I'll call him Mark. "Lady, don't waste your time," he told me. "We're the retards." Then Mark strolled out of the room.

Dumbstruck, I slumped into my chair and wondered if I should have become a teacher. Was the only cure for problems like this to get out? I told myself I'd suffer for one year, and after my marriage that next summer I'd do something more rewarding.

"They got to you, didn't they?" It was my colleague who had come into my classroom earlier. I nodded.

"Don't worry," he said. "I taught many of them in summer school. There are only 14 of them, and most won't graduate anyway. Don't waste your time with those kids."

"What do you mean?"

"They live in shacks in the fields. They're migratory labor, pickers' kids. They come to school only when they feel like it. The boy on the floor had pestered Mark's sister while they were picking beans together. I had to tell them to shut up at lunch today. Just keep them busy and quiet. If they cause any trouble, send them to me."

As I gathered my things to go home, I couldn't forget the look on Mark's face as he said, "We're the retards." *Retards*. That word clattered in my brain. I knew I had to do something drastic.

The next afternoon I asked my colleague not to come into my class again. I needed to handle the kids in my own way. I returned to my room and made eye contact with each student. Then I went to the board and wrote *ECINAJ*.

"That's my first name," I said. "Can you tell me what it is?"

They told me my name was "weird" and that they had never seen it before. I went to the board again and this time wrote *JANICE*. Several of them blurted the word, then gave me a funny look.

"You're right, my name is Janice," I said. "I'm learning-impaired, something called dyslexia. When I began school I couldn't write my own name correctly. I couldn't spell words, and numbers swam in my head.

I was labeled 'retarded.' That's right—I was a 'retard.' I can still hear those awful voices and feel the shame."

"So how'd you become a teacher?" someone asked.

"Because I hate labels and I'm not stupid and I love to learn. That's what this class is going to be about. If you like the label 'retard,' then you don't belong here. Change classes. There are no retarded people in this room.

"I'm not going to be easy on you," I continued. "We're going to work and work until you catch up. You *will* graduate, and I hope some of you will go on to college. That's not a joke—it's a promise. I don't *ever* want to hear the word 'retard' in this room again. Do you understand?"

They seemed to sit up a little straighter.

We did work hard, and I soon caught glimpses of promise. Mark, especially, was very bright. I heard him tell a boy in the hall, "This book's real good. We don't read baby books in there." He was holding a copy of *To Kill a Mockingbird*.

Months flew by, and the improvement was wonderful. Then one day Mark said, "But people still think we're stupid 'cause we don't talk right." It was the moment I had been waiting for. Now we could begin an intensive study of grammar, because they wanted it.

I was sorry to see the month of June approach; they wanted to learn so much. All my students knew I was getting married and moving out of state. The students in my last-period class were visibly agitated whenever I mentioned it. I was glad they had become fond of me, but what was wrong? Were they angry I was leaving the school?

On my final day of classes, the principal greeted me as I entered the building. "Will you come with me, please?" he said sternly. "There's a problem with your room." He looked straight ahead as he led me down the hall. *What now?* I wondered.

It was amazing! There were sprays of flowers in each corner, bouquets on the students' desks and filing cabinets, and a huge blanket of flowers lying on my desk. *How could they have done this?* I wondered. Most of them were so poor that they relied on the school assistance program for warm clothing and decent meals.

I started to cry, and they joined me.

Later I learned how they had pulled it off. Mark, who worked in the local flower shop on weekends, had seen orders from several of my other classes. He mentioned them to his classmates. Too proud to ever again wear an insulting label like "poor," Mark had asked the florist for all the "tired" flowers in the shop. Then he called funeral parlors and explained that his class needed flowers for a teacher who was leaving. They agreed to give him bouquets saved after each funeral.

That was not the only tribute they paid me, though. Two years later, all 14 students graduated, and six earned college scholarships.

Twenty-eight years later, I'm teaching in an academically strong school not too far from where I began my career. I learned that Mark married his college sweetheart and is a successful businessman. And, coincidentally, three years ago Mark's son was in my sophomore honors English class.

Sometimes I laugh when I recall the end of my first day as a teacher. To think I considered quitting to do something *rewarding!*

Janice Anderson Connolly

A Scoutmaster Saves the Day

For weeks the troop had been engaged in expectant preparation for its Parents' Night program. Everything was in order. The walls were filled with displays, the scouts with enthusiasm and the tables with good things to eat.

The toastmaster was well under way. The crowd sang with that respectably restrained enthusiasm that typified a Parents' Night program.

Then Jimmie Davis arose to give his oration. This was the moment he had looked forward to for many weeks. As he arose, he caught a glimpse of his mother's beaming face and his father's stolid assured countenance. He started with a great burst of enthusiasm. He waxed more eloquent, conscious that his listeners were paying a high tribute to him by their careful attention.

Then something happened. The world seemed to swim before him. He slowed down—faltered—stopped. His face flushed, his hands sought each other frantically and in desperation he looked helplessly toward his scoutmaster.

And ever prepared, having heard that boyish masterpiece rehearsed again and again, the boy's leader supplied the missing words and the lad went on. But somehow it was different now. The masterpiece had been marred.

Jimmie paused again—and the scoutmaster prompted him again. For the remaining two minutes, the oration seemed more the scoutmaster's than the boy's.

But Jimmie finished it. In the heart of the lad who sat down, knowing that he had failed, there was a heavy load. Chagrin was plainly written on the face of the boy's mother, and a twitch of the father's face indicated a pained consciousness of shame.

The audience applauded in a perfunctory way, sorry for and pitying the boy who they thought had failed.

But the scoutmaster was on his feet. His quiet eyes twinkled. All listened tensely, for he did not talk loudly. What was he saying?

"I am more happy than any of you can possibly understand because of what has just happened. You have seen a boy make a glorious victory out of what might have been a miserable failure.

"Jimmie had his chance to quit. To have quit would have been easy. But to finish the job even in the face of 200 people required the highest kind of bravery and courage I know.

"You may someday hear a better oratorical effect, but I am confident that you will never see a finer demonstration of the spirit of our troop than Jimmie has just given you—to play the game even under difficulties!"

The people thundered their applause now. Jimmie's mother sat straight and proud. The old look of assurance was back on the face of the boy's father. The entire group was enthusiastic again and Jimmie, with a lump in his throat, said something to the friend beside him that sounded like, "Gee, if I can be that kind of a scoutmaster someday."

Walter MacPeek
Submitted by Martin Louw

What's Happening
with Today's Youth?

If you treat an individual . . . as if he were
what he ought to be and could be, he will
become what he ought to be and could be.

Goethe

Our young people are growing up much faster today. They need our help.

But what could I do?

My inner voice questioned me as to why I wasn't a role model for today's generation of young people. No, I couldn't do that. I wasn't a psychologist and I sure didn't have the type of influence to create massive change like a politician.

I'm an engineer. I obtained my degree in electrical engineering from the University of Virginia. Now I work for Hewlett-Packard.

But the thought wouldn't leave me.

So finally, I decided to do something. That morning, I called up the local neighborhood high school. I spoke to the principal, sharing my desire to help. He was thrilled and invited me to come down during lunch. I agreed.

At noon, I drove to the school. Many thoughts bombarded my mind: "Can I relate to them? Do students want to talk to an outsider?"

I hadn't been on a high school campus for quite a few years. As I walked down the hallway, students were buzzing with excitement. It was crowded. Students looked much older to me. Most of them were wearing baggy clothes.

Finally, I made it to the classroom, Room 103, where I was to share some insight with the students. I took a deep breath and opened the door. There, I found 32 students chit-chatting. As I walked in, everything stopped. All eyes were on me. "Hi, I'm Marlon."

"Hey, Marlon, come on in." SHOOOOOOO, a moment of relief came over me. They accepted me.

During that one-hour session, we had fun talking about goal-setting, the importance of school, and con-flict resolution without violence. When the bell rang signaling time for the next class, I didn't want it to end. Time just flew by and before we knew it, it was already time for me to return to work. I couldn't believe how much fun I had. I went back to work pumped up.

This continued for months. I developed many rela-tionships at the school. Most students bonded to me. But not all the students were excited about my coming.

In fact, there was Paul.

I'll never forget Paul. He was a real tough-looking guy, about 6'2", 220 lbs. He had just transferred to this school. Rumor had it that he had been in and out of many juvenile detention centers. In fact, the teachers were scared of him. And why not? Two years ago, he had been sentenced for stabbing his English teacher in the chest during an argument. Everyone let him do what he wanted. He strolled to class late. Never carried a book in hand because he was just too cool for school.

From time to time, he sat in on my lunch sessions but never said anything. I think the only reason he came was to "check out the babes."

Whenever I tried to get him involved, he just stared at me with his piercing eyes. He intimidated me. He was like a bomb just waiting to explode. But I wasn't going to give up on him. Every time he came, I tried to engage him in the discussion, but he wasn't interested.

One day, I had enough and the bomb exploded.

During this particular session, we were developing our "goals collage." Students were cutting out pictures of their goals from magazines and pasting them onto a poster board. We were 20 minutes into the session when Paul strolled in.

I asked for a volunteer to share his or her goals collage with the rest of the class. Julie, a petite girl, stood up and began sharing her dreams. I was happy to see Julie stand up because, when I first met her, she was so shy.

"I'm going to go to medical school to become a doctor."

All of a sudden, laughter broke out from the back of the room.

"Please. You, a doctor? Be for real. You ain't gonna be anybody."

All heads turned to the back of the room. Paul was laughing at his statement.

I was shocked. I couldn't believe what just took place. There was complete silence. What should I do? My adrenaline was flowing strong.

"Paul, that's not right. Who are you to put somebody else down?"

"Yo, teach, you dissin' me? Are you disrespecting me? Do you know who I am? Look man, I'm an O.G., Original Gangster. Don't mess with me; you'll get hurt."

He started walking toward the door.

"No, Paul, that doesn't fly. You have no right to put somebody else down. Enough is enough. You don't have to be here. Either you're part of the group or you're not. We've got a team here that supports one another. And, Paul, you have so much potential. We want your participation. You have so much to offer the group. I care about you and this entire group. That's why I'm here. Are you going to be a team player?"

Paul looked over his shoulder and gave me a stare of terror. He opened the door and walked out, slamming the door behind him.

The class was shaken by this drama, and so was I.

After class, I packed up my materials and started making my way to the parking lot. As I approached my car, someone called out to me.

I turned around and to my surprise, it was Paul. He was walking quickly toward me. A state of fear came over me. Part of me wanted to get help, but it happened so fast that I couldn't move.

"Mr. Smith, you remember what you said to me?"

"Yeah, Paul."

"Did you mean what you said about caring for me and wanting me to be part of the team?"

"Yeah, of course, Paul."

"Well, no one has ever in my life told me that they care for me. You are the first person to ever say that. I want to be part of the team. Thanks for caring enough to stand up to me. I'll apologize to Julie tomorrow in front of the entire class."

I couldn't believe my ears. I was in shock. I could hardly speak.

As he walked away, tears of joy swelled up in my eyes and started rolling down my face. I had been truly touched for life. That day I decided to commit my life to empowering our young people to realize their true potential.

Marlon Smith

Cipher in the Snow

It started with tragedy on a biting cold February morning. I was driving behind the Milford Corners bus as I did most snowy mornings on my way to school. It veered and stopped short at the hotel, which it had no business doing, and I was annoyed as I had to come to an unexpected stop. A boy lurched out of the bus, reeled, stumbled and collapsed on the snow bank at the curb. The bus driver and I reached him at the same moment. His thin, hollow face was white even against the snow.

"He's dead," the driver whispered.

It didn't register for a minute. I glanced quickly at the scared young faces staring down at us from the school bus. "A doctor! Quick! I'll phone from the hotel."

"No use. I tell you, he's dead." The driver looked down at the boy's still form. "He never even said he felt bad," he muttered, "just tapped me on the shoulder and said, real quiet, 'I'm sorry. I have to get off at the hotel.' That's all. Polite and apologizing like."

At school, the giggling, shuffling morning noise quieted as the news went down the halls. I passed a huddle of girls. "Who was it? Who dropped dead on the way to school?" I heard one of them half whisper.

"Don't know his name; some kid from Milford Corners," was the reply.

It was like that in the faculty room and the principal's office. "I'd appreciate you going out to tell the parents," the principal told me. "They haven't a phone, and anyway, somebody from school should go there in person. I'll cover your classes."

"Why me?" I asked. "Wouldn't it be better if you did it?"

"I didn't know the boy," the principal admitted levelly. "And in last year's sophomore personalities column I noticed that you were listed as his favorite teacher."

I drove through the snow and cold down the bad canyon road to the Evans' place and thought about the boy, Cliff Evans. His favorite teacher! Why, he hadn't spoken two words to me in two years! I could see him in my mind's eye all right, sitting back there in the last seat in my afternoon literature class. He came in the room by himself and left by himself. "Cliff Evans," I muttered to myself, "a boy who never smiled. I never saw him smile once."

The big ranch kitchen was clean and warm. I blurted out my news somehow. Mrs. Evans reached blindly for a chair. "He never said anything about bein' ailing."

His stepfather snorted. "He ain't said nothin' about anything since I moved in here."

Mrs. Evans got up, pushed a pan to the back of the stove and began to untie her apron. "Now hold on," her husband snapped. "I got to have breakfast before I go to town. Nothin' we can do now anyway. If Cliff hadn't been so dumb, he'd have told us he didn't feel good."

After school I sat in the office and stared bleakly at the records spread out before me. I was to close the boy's file and write his obituary for the school paper. The almost bare sheets mocked the effort. "Cliff Evans, white, never legally adopted by stepfather, five half-brothers and sisters." These meager strands of information and the list of D grades were about all the records had to offer.

Cliff Evans had silently come in the school door in the mornings and gone out the school door in the evenings, and that was all. He had never belonged to a club. He had never played on a team. He had never held an office. As far as I could tell, he had never done one happy, noisy kid thing. He had never been anybody at all.

How do you go about making a boy into a zero? The grade-school records showed me much of the answer. The first- and second-grade teachers' annotations read "sweet, shy child; timid but eager." Then the third grade note had opened the attack. Some teacher had written in a good, firm hand, "Cliff won't talk. Uncooperative. Slow learner." The other academic sheep had followed with "dull," "slow-witted," "low IQ." They became correct. The boy's IQ score in the ninth grade listed at 83. But his IQ in the third grade had been 106. The score didn't go under 100 until the seventh grade. Even timid, sweet children have resilience. It takes time to break them.

I stomped to the typewriter and wrote a savage report pointing out what education had done to Cliff Evans. I slapped a copy on the principal's desk and another in the sad, dog-eared file, slammed the file and crashed the office door shut as I left for home. But I didn't feel much better. A little boy kept walking after me, a boy with a peaked face, a skinny body in faded jeans, and big eyes that had searched for a long time and then had become veiled.

I could guess how many times he'd been chosen last to be on a team, how many whispered child conversations had excluded him. I could see the faces and hear the voices that said over and over, "You're dumb. You're dumb. You're just a nothing, Cliff Evans."

A child is a believing creature. Cliff undoubtedly believed them. Suddenly it seemed clear to me: When finally there was nothing left at all for Cliff Evans, he collapsed on a snow bank and went away. The doctor might list "heart failure" as the cause of death, but that wouldn't change my mind.

Jean Tod Hunter

Reprinted by permission of Jean Tod Hunter

A Simple Touch

My friend Charlie let himself in, back door slamming. He made a beeline for my refrigerator, searched out a Budweiser and slid into a kitchen chair. I regarded him with interest.

He had that shaken, bewildered look of someone who had just seen a ghost or maybe had confronted his own mortality. His eyes were rimmed with darkness and he kept waving his head from side to side as if carrying on a conversation inside himself. Finally he took a long swig of the beer and made eye contact.

I told him he looked pretty awful. He acknowledged that, adding that he felt even worse, *shaken*. Then he told me his remarkable story.

Charlie is an art teacher at a local high school. He has been there for many years and enjoys the envied reputation of one who is respected by colleagues and sought out by students. It seems that on this particular day he had been visited by a former student, returning after four or five years to show off her wedding ring, her new baby and her budding career.

Charlie stopped talking long enough to taste his beer. So, that was it, I thought. He had confronted his own mortality. The years fly past for a teacher and it is always disconcerting to blink and find a woman where only yesterday there had been a child.

"No, that wasn't it, exactly," Charlie informed me. "Not a lesson in mortality. Not a ghost." It had been a lesson, he explained, in humility.

The visitor, Angela, had been a semi-serious art student nearly five years earlier. Charlie remembered her as a quiet, plain girl who mostly kept to herself, but who welcomed friendly overtures with shy smiles.

Now she was a confident young woman, a mother, who initiated conversations instead of responding to them. She had come to see her former art teacher and she had an agenda. She began after only a few preliminary amenities.

"When I was in high school," she explained, "my stepfather abused me. He hit me and he came into my bed at night. It was horrible. I was deeply ashamed. I told no one. No one knew.

"Finally, during my junior year, my parents went away for the weekend, leaving me home alone for the first time. I planned my escape.

"They left on Thursday evening, so I spent the entire night preparing. I did my homework, wrote a long letter to my mother, and organized my belongings. I purchased a roll of wide plastic tape and spent an hour taping all the outside doors and windows of the garage from the inside. I put the keys in the ignition of my mother's car, put my teddy bear on the passenger's seat and then went up to bed.

"My plan was to go to school as usual on Friday and ride the bus home, as usual. I would wait at home until my parents called, talk to them, then go to the garage and start the engine. I figured nobody would find me until Sunday afternoon when my parents returned. I would be dead. I would be free."

Angela had held to her plan until eighth-period art class, when Charlie, her art teacher, perched on the stool next to her, examined her artwork and slipped an arm around her shoulder. He made small talk, listened to the answer, squeezed her lightly and moved on.

Angela had gone home that Friday afternoon and written a second, different letter of good-bye to her mother. She removed the tape from the garage and packed her teddy bear with the rest of her belongings. Then she called her minister, who immediately came for her. She left her parents' home and never went back. She flourished and she gave Charlie the credit.

The story nearing its end, Charlie and I shared some quiet conversation about schools that warn teachers not to touch students, about the philosophy that social time in schools is wasted time, about how sheer numbers of students sometimes preclude this type of encounter. How many times, we wondered, had we flippantly related to students in need? We sat in silence then, soaking up the intensity and implications of such a story. This type of encounter must happen thousands of times in schools and churches and shopping malls every day. It was nothing special. Adults like Charlie do it naturally, without thinking.

Then Charlie gave his interpretation. Angela had decided in that moment, in that art class, that if a casually friendly teacher cared enough about her to take the time to stop, make contact, look at her and listen to her, then there must be other people who cared about her, too. She could find them.

Charlie put his head in his hands while I rubbed the gooseflesh from my arms. He looked up at me, armed with his new lesson in humility. "Nancy," he said very quietly, very emphatically, "what humbles me the most is that I don't even remember the incident!"

And all these years later, she had come back to tell him that she credited him with saving her life.

Nancy Moorman

Adam

While recuperating from her second open heart surgery at Children's Hospital of Western Ontario, my six-year-old daughter Kelley was moved from the intensive care unit to the floor with the other children. Because a section of the floor was closed, Kelley was put in the wing reserved for cancer patients.

In the adjacent room, a six-year-old boy named Adam was fighting a battle with leukemia. Adam stayed at the hospital for a portion of each month while receiving chemotherapy treatments. Every day Adam sauntered into Kelley's room to visit, pushing the pole that held his chemotherapy bag. Despite the discomfort of the treatments, Adam was always smiling and cheerful. He entertained us for hours with his many stories. Adam had a way of finding the positive and the humor in any situation, however difficult.

One particular day, I was feeling tired and anxious for Kelley's release from the hospital. The gray, gloomy day outside only fueled my poor mood. While I stood at the window looking at the rainy sky, Adam came in for his daily visit. I commented to him on what a depressing day it was. With his ever-present smile, Adam turned to me and cheerily replied, "Every day is beautiful for me."

From that day on I have never had a gloomy day. Even the grayest days bring a feeling of joy as I remember with gratitude the words of wisdom spoken by a very brave six-year-old boy named Adam.

—*Patty Merritt*

Reprinted by permission of Patty Merritt. ©1995 Patty Merritt.

Miss Hardy

There comes that mysterious meeting in life when someone acknowledges who we are and what we can be, igniting the circuits of our highest potential.

Rusty Berkus

I began life as a learning-disabled child. I had a distortion of vision called *dyslexia*. Dyslexic children often learn words quickly, but don't know they don't see them the way other people do. I perceived my world as a wonderful place filled with these shapes called words and developed a rather extensive sight vocabulary that made my parents quite optimistic about my ability to learn. To my horror, I discovered in the first grade that letters were more important than words. Dyslexic children make them upside down and backwards, and don't even arrange them in the same order as everybody else. So my first-grade teacher called me learning-disabled.

She wrote down her observations and passed them on to my second-grade teacher over the summer so she could develop an appropriate bias against me before I arrived. I entered the second grade able to see the answers to math problems but having no idea what the busy work was to reach them, and discovered that the busy work was more important than the answer. Now I was totally intimidated by the learning process, so I developed a stutter. Being unable to speak up assertively, unable to perform normal math functions and arranging letters inappropriately, I was a complete disaster. I developed the strategy of moving to the back of each class, staying out of sight and, when apprehended and called upon, muttering or mumbling, "I d-d-don't kn-kn-know." That sealed my fate.

My third-grade teacher knew before I arrived that I couldn't speak, write, read or do mathematics, so she had no real optimism toward dealing with me. I discovered malingering as a basic tool to get through school. This allowed me to spend more time with the school nurse than the teacher or find vague reasons to stay home or be sent home. That was my strategy in the third and fourth grades.

Just as I was about to die intellectually, I entered the fifth grade and God placed me under the tutelage of the awesome Miss Hardy, known in the western United States as one of the most formidable elementary school teachers ever to walk the Rocky Mountains. This incredible woman, whose six-foot-frame towered above me, put her arms around me and said, "He's not learning-disabled, he's eccentric."

Now, people view the potential of an eccentric child far more optimistically than a plain old disabled one. But she didn't leave it there. She said, "I've talked with your mother and she says when she reads something to you, you remember it almost photographically. You just don't do it well when you're asked to assemble all the words and pieces. And reading out loud appears to be a problem, so when I'm going to call on you to read in my class, I'll let you know in advance so you can go home and memorize it the night before, then we'll fake it in front of the other kids. Also, Mom says when you look something over, you can talk about it with great understanding, but when she asks you to read it word for word and even write something about it, you appear to get hung up in the letters and stuff and lose the meaning. So, when the other kids are asked to read and write those worksheets I give them, you can go home and under less pressure on your own time do them and bring them back to me the next day."

She also said, "I notice you appear to be hesitant and fearful to express your thoughts and I believe that any idea a person has is worth considering. I've looked into this and I'm not sure it will work, but it helped a man named Demosthenes—can you say Demosthenes?"

"D-d-d-d . . ."

She said, "Well, you will be able to. He had an unruly tongue, so he put stones in his mouth and practiced until he got control of it. So I've got a couple of marbles, too big for you to swallow, that I've washed off. From now on when I call on you, I'd like you to put them in your mouth and stand up and speak up until I can hear and understand you." And, of course, supported by her manifest belief in and understanding of me I took the risk, tamed my tongue, and was able to speak.

The next year I went on to the sixth grade, and to my delight, so did Miss Hardy. So I had the opportunity to spend two full years under her tutelage.

I kept track of Miss Hardy over the years and learned a few years ago that she was terminally ill with cancer. Knowing how lonely she would be with her only special student over 1,000 miles away, I naively bought a plane ticket and traveled all that distance to stand in line (at least figuratively) behind several hundred other of her special students—people who had also kept track of her and had made a pilgrimage to renew their association and share their affection for her in the latter period of her life. The group was a very interesting mix of people—3 U.S. Senators, 12 state legislators and a number of chief executive officers of corporations and businesses.

The interesting thing, in comparing notes, is that three-fourths of us went into the fifth grade quite intimidated by the educational process, believing we were incapable, insignificant and at the mercy of fate or luck. We emerged from our contact with Miss Hardy believing we were capable, significant, influential people who had the capacity to make a difference in life if we would try.

H. Stephen Glenn

As a Man Soweth

When I was in junior high, the eighth-grade bully punched me in the stomach. Not only did it hurt and make me angry, but the embarrassment and humiliation were almost intolerable. I wanted desperately to even the score! I planned to meet him by the bike racks the next day and let him have it.

For some reason, I told my plan to Nana, my grandmother—big mistake. She gave me one of her hour-long lectures (that woman could really talk). The lecture was a total drag, but among other things, I vaguely remember her telling me that I didn't need to worry about him. She said, "Good deeds beget good results, and evil deeds beget bad results." I told her, in a nice way, of course, that I thought she was full of it. I told her that I did good things all the time, and all I got in return was "baloney!" (I didn't use that word.) She stuck to her guns, though. She said, "Every good deed will come back to you someday, and every bad thing you do will also come back to you."

It took me 30 years to understand the wisdom of her words. Nana was living in a board-and-care home in Laguna Hills, California. Each Tuesday, I came by and took her out to dinner. I would always find her neatly dressed and sitting in a chair right by the front door. I vividly remember our very last dinner together before she went into the convalescent hospital. We drove to a nearby simple little family-owned restaurant. I ordered pot roast for Nana and a hamburger for myself. The food arrived and as I dug in, I noticed that Nana wasn't eating. She was just staring at the food on her plate. Moving my plate aside, I took Nana's plate, placed it in front of me, and cut her meat into small pieces. I then placed the plate back in front of her. As she very weakly, and with great difficulty, forked the meat into her mouth, I was struck with a memory that brought instant tears to my eyes. Forty years previously, as a little boy sitting at the table, Nana had always taken the meat on my plate and cut it into small pieces so I could eat it.

It had taken 40 years, but the good deed had been repaid. Nana was right. We reap exactly what we sow. "Every good deed you do will someday come back to you."

What about the eighth-grade bully?

He ran into the ninth-grade bully.

Mike Buettell

6

LIVE
YOUR
DREAM

*T*he future belongs to those
who believe in the beauty of
their dreams.

Eleanor Roosevelt

A Small Boy

A small boy
Looked at a star
And began to weep.
And
The star said
Boy
Why are you weeping?
And
The boy said
You are so far away
I will never be able
To touch you
And
The star answered
Boy
If I were not already
In your heart
You would not be able
To see me.

John Magliola

A Little Girl's Dream

The promise was a long time keeping. But then, so was the dream.

In the early 1950s in a small Southern California town, a little girl hefted yet another load of books onto the tiny library's counter.

The girl was a reader. Her parents had books all over their home, but not always the ones she wanted. So she'd make her weekly trek to the yellow library with the brown trim, the little one-room building where the children's library actually was just a nook. Frequently, she ventured out of that nook in search of heftier fare.

As the white-haired librarian hand-stamped the due dates in the 10-year-old's choices, the little girl looked longingly at "The New Book" prominently displayed on the counter. She marveled again at the wonder of writing a book and having it honored like that, right there for the world to see.

That particular day, she confessed her goal.

"When I grow up," she said, "I'm going to be a writer. I'm going to write books."

The librarian looked up from her stamping and smiled, not with the condescension so many children receive, but with encouragement.

"When you do write that book," she replied, "bring it into our library and we'll put it on display, right here on the counter."

The little girl promised she would.

As she grew, so did her dream. She got her first job in ninth grade, writing brief personality profiles, which earned her $1.50 each from the local newspaper. The money palled in comparison with the magic of seeing her words on paper.

A book was a long way off.

She edited her high-school paper, married and started a family, but the itch to write burned deep. She got a part-time job covering school news at a weekly newspaper. It kept her brain busy as she balanced babies.

But no book.

She went to work full-time for a major daily. Even tried her hand at magazines.

Still no book.

Finally, she believed she had something to say and started a book. She sent it off to two publishers and was rejected. She put it away, sadly. Several years later, the old dream increased in persistence. She got an agent and wrote another book. She pulled the other out of hiding, and soon both were sold.

But the world of book publishing moves slower than that of daily newspapers, and she waited two long years. The day the box arrived on her doorstep with its free author's copies, she ripped it open. Then she cried. She'd waited so long to hold her dream in her hands.

Then she remembered that librarian's invitation, and her promise.

Of course, that particular librarian had died long ago, and the little library had been razed to make way for a larger incarnation.

The woman called and got the name of the head librarian. She wrote a letter, telling her how much her predecessor's words had meant to the girl. She'd be in town for her 30th high school reunion, she wrote, and could she please bring her two books by and give them to the library? It would mean so much to that ten-year-old girl, and seemed a way of honoring all the librarians who had ever encouraged a child.

The librarian called and said, "Come." So she did, clutching a copy of each book.

She found the big new library right across the street from her old high school; just opposite the room where she'd struggled through algebra, mourning the necessity of a subject that writers would surely never use, and nearly on top of the spot where her old house once stood, the neighborhood demolished for a civic center and this looming library.

Inside, the librarian welcomed her warmly. She introduced a reporter from the local newspaper—a descendant of the paper she'd begged a chance to write for long ago.

Then she presented her books to the librarian, who placed them on the counter with a sign of explanation. Tears rolled down the woman's cheeks.

Then she hugged the librarian and left, pausing for a picture outside, which proved that dreams can come true and promises can be kept. Even if it takes 38 years.

The ten-year-old girl and the writer she'd become posed by the library sign, right next to the reader-board, which said:

WELCOME BACK,
JANN MITCHELL

Jann Mitchell

A Salesman's First Sale

Keep away from people who try to belittle your ambitions. Small people always do that, but the really great make you feel that you, too, can become great.

Mark Twain

I hurried home one Saturday afternoon in the fall of 1993 to try to get some much-needed yard work done. While raking leaves, my five-year-old son, Nick, came over and pulled on my pants leg. "Dad, I need you to make me a sign," he said.

"Not now, Nick, I'm real busy," was my reply.

"But I need a sign," he persisted.

"What for, Nick?" I asked.

"I'm going to sell some of my rocks," was his answer.

Nick has always been fascinated with rocks and stones. He's collected them from all over, and people bring them to him. There is a basket full of rocks in the garage that he periodically cleans, sorts and restacks. They are his treasures. "I don't have time to mess with it right now, Nick. I have to get these leaves raked," I said. "Go have your mom help you."

A short while later, Nick returned with a sheet of paper. On it, in his five-year-old handwriting, were the words "ON SALE TODAY, $1.00." His mom had helped him make his sign, and he was now in business. He took his sign, a small basket and four of his best rocks and walked to the end of our driveway. There he arranged the rocks in a line, set the basket behind them and sat down. I watched from the distance, amused at his determination.

After half an hour or so, not a single person had passed by. I walked down the drive to see how he was doing. "How's it going, Nick?" I asked.

"Good," he replied.

"What's the basket for?" I asked.

"To put the money in," was his matter-of-fact answer.

"How much are you asking for your rocks?"

"A dollar each," Nick said.

"Nick, nobody will pay you a dollar for a rock."

"Yes, they will!"

"Nick, there isn't enough traffic on our street for people to see your rocks. Why don't you pack these up and go play?"

"Yes, there is, Dad," he countered. "People walk and ride their bikes on our street for exercise, and some people drive their cars to look at the houses. There's enough people."

Having failed to convince Nick of the futility of his efforts, I went back to my yard work. He patiently remained at his post. A short while later, a mini-van came driving down the street. I watched as Nick perked up, holding his sign up and pointing it at the van. As it slowly passed, I saw a young couple craning their necks to read his sign. They continued on around the cul-de-sac and as they approached Nick again, the lady rolled down her window. I couldn't hear the conversation, but she turned to the man driving and I could see him reaching for his billfold! He handed her a dollar and she got out of the van and walked over to Nick. After examining the rocks, she picked up one, gave Nick the dollar and then drove off.

I sat in the yard, amazed, as Nick ran up to me. Waving the dollar, he shouted, "I told you I could sell one rock for a dollar—if you believe in yourself, you can do anything!" I went and got my camera and took a picture of Nick and his sign. The little guy had held tough to his belief and delighted in showing what he could do. It was a great lesson in how not to raise children, but we all learned from it and talk about it to this day.

Later that day, my wife, Toni, Nick and I went out to dinner. On the way, Nick asked us if he could have an allowance. His mom explained that an allowance must be earned and we would have to determine what his responsibilities would be. "That's okay," said Nick, "how much will I get?"

"At five years old, how about a dollar a week?" said Toni.

From the backseat came, "A dollar a week—I can make that selling one rock!"

Rob, Toni and Nick Harris

Let's Walk Through the Garden Again

It is one of the most beautiful compensations of this life that no man can sincerely try to help another without helping himself.

Ralph Waldo Emerson

I am a public speaker who teaches fellow Canadians creative ways to buy real estate. One of my very first graduates, a policeman named Roy, used my ideas in a most touching way.

The story begins years before Roy attended my course. On his regular rounds, he was in the habit of dropping in on an elderly gentleman who lived in a breathtaking 5,000-square-foot mansion overlooking a ravine. The older man had lived there most of his life and cherished the view, the many mature trees and the creek.

When Roy would check in on him, once or twice a week, the old man would offer him tea and they would sit and chat or stroll for a few minutes through the garden. One such visit was sad. The older man tearfully admitted that his health was failing and he had to sell his beautiful home and move into a nursing home.

By this time, Roy had taken my course and came up with the crazy idea that he might be able to use the creativity of my course to figure out how to buy this mansion.

The man wanted $300,000 for his home, which had no mortgage. Roy had only $3,000 in savings. Roy was paying $500 in rent at the time and he had a reasonable policeman's salary. It seemed insurmountable to come up with a plan to create a deal between the man and the hopeful policeman . . . insurmountable until you take into account the power of love.

Roy remembered the words of my course—to find out what the vendor truly wants and give it to him. After delving as deeply as he could, Roy finally found the key. What the man was going to miss the most was walking through his garden.

Roy blurted out: "If you let me buy your house, somehow, I promise to pick you up one or two Sundays a month, bring you back here to your garden and let you sit here and stroll around it with me, like old times."

The old man smiled in wonder and love. The old man told Roy to write up whatever offer seemed fair and he'd sign it. Roy offered all he could afford. The purchase price was $300,000. The downpayment was $3,000. The vendor took back a $297,000 first mortgage bearing interest at $500 a month. The old man was so happy that, as a present, he let Roy have all the antique furniture in the whole house, including a baby grand piano.

As amazed as Roy was at his incredible financial victory, the real winner was the happy old man and the relationship that the two of them shared.

Raymond L. Aaron

18 Holes in His Mind

Major James Nesmeth had a dream of improving his golf game—and he developed a unique method of achieving his goal. Until he devised this method, he was just your average weekend golfer, shooting in the mid- to low-nineties. Then, for seven years, he completely quit the game. Never touched a club. Never set foot on a fairway.

Ironically, it was during this seven-year break from the game that Major Nesmeth came up with his amazingly effective technique for improving his game—a technique we can all learn from. In fact, the first time he set foot on a golf course after his hiatus from the game, he shot an astonishing 74! He had cut 20 strokes off his average without having swung a golf club in seven years! Unbelievable. Not only that, but his physical condition had actually deteriorated during those seven years.

What was Major Nesmeth's secret? Visualization.

You see, Major Nesmeth had spent those seven years as a prisoner of war in North Vietnam. During those seven years, he was imprisoned in a cage that was approximately four and one-half feet high and five feet long.

During almost the entire time he was imprisoned, he saw no one, talked to no one and experienced no physical activity. During the first few months he did virtually nothing but hope and pray for his release. Then he realized he had to find some way to occupy his mind or he would lose his sanity and probably his life. That's when he learned to visualize.

In his mind, he selected his favorite golf course and started playing golf. Every day, he played a full 18 holes at the imaginary country club of his dreams. He experienced everything to the last detail. He saw himself dressed in his golfing clothes. He smelled the fragrance of the trees and the freshly trimmed grass. He experienced different weather conditions—windy spring days, overcast winter days, and sunny summer mornings. In his imagination, every detail of the tee, the individual blades of grass, the trees, the singing birds, the scampering squirrels and the lay of the course became totally real.

He felt the grip of the club in his hands. He instructed himself as he practiced smoothing out his down-swing and the follow-through on his shot. Then he watched the ball arc down the exact center of the fairway, bounce a couple of times and roll to the exact spot he had selected, all in his mind.

In the real world, he was in no hurry. He had no place to go. So in his mind he took every step on his way to the ball, just as if he were physically on the course. It took him just as long in imaginary time to play 18 holes as it would have taken in reality. Not a detail was omitted. Not once did he ever miss a shot, never a hook or a slice, never a missed putt.

Seven days a week. Four hours a day. Eighteen holes. Seven years. Twenty strokes off. Shot a 74.

Author Unknown

Keep Your Goals in Sight

When she looked ahead, Florence Chadwick saw nothing but a solid wall of fog. Her body was numb. She had been swimming for nearly sixteen hours.

Already she was the first woman to swim the English Channel in both directions. Now, at age 34, her goal was to become the first woman to swim from Catalina Island to the California coast.

On that Fourth of July morning in 1952, the sea was like an ice bath and the fog was so dense she could hardly see her support boats. Sharks cruised toward her lone figure, only to be driven away by rifle shots. Against the frigid grip of the sea, she struggled on— hour after hour—while millions watched on national television.

Alongside Florence in one of the boats, her mother and her trainer offered encouragement. They told her it wasn't much farther. But all she could see was fog. They urged her not to quit. She never had . . . until then. With only a half mile to go, she asked to be pulled out.

Still thawing her chilled body several hours later, she told a reporter, "Look, I'm not excusing myself, but if I could have *seen* land I might have made it." It was not fatigue or even the cold water that defeated her. It was the fog. *She was unable to see her goal.*

Two months later, she tried again. This time, despite the same dense fog, she swam with her faith intact and her goal clearly pictured in her mind. She knew that somewhere behind that fog was land and this time she made it! Florence Chadwick became the first woman to swim the Catalina Channel, eclipsing the men's record by two hours!

Author Unknown
Submitted by Michele Borba

The Cowboy's Story

When I started my telecommunications company, I knew I was going to need salespeople to help me expand the business. I put the word out that I was looking for qualified salespeople and began the interviewing process. The salesperson I had in mind was experienced in the telemarketing communications industry, knew the local market, had experience with the various types of systems available, had a professional demeanor and was a self-starter. I had very little time to train a person, so it was important that the salesperson I hired could "hit the ground running."

During the tiresome process of interviewing prospective salespeople, into my office walked a cowboy. I knew he was a cowboy by the way he was dressed. He had on corduroy pants and a corduroy jacket that didn't match the pants; a short-sleeved snap-button shirt; a tie that came about halfway down his chest with a knot bigger than my fist; cowboy boots; and a baseball cap. You can imagine what I was thinking: "Not what I had in mind for my new company." He sat down in front of my desk, took off his cap and said, "Mister, I'd just shore appreciate a chance to be a success in the telephone biness." And that's just how he said it, too: *biness.*

I was trying to figure out a way to tell this fellow, without being too blunt, that he just wasn't what I had in mind at all. I asked him about his background. He said he had a degree in agriculture from Oklahoma State University and that he had been a ranch hand in Bartlesville, Oklahoma, for the past few years during the summers. He announced that was all over now, he was ready to be a success in "biness," and he would just "shore appreciate a chance."

We continued to talk. He was so focused on success and how he would "shore appreciate a chance" that I decided to give him a chance. I told him that I would spend two days with him. In those two days I would teach him everything I thought he needed to know to sell one type of very small telephone system. At the end of those two days he would be on his own. He asked me how much money I thought he could make.

I told him, "Looking like you look and knowing what you know, the best you can do is about $1,000 per month." I went on to explain that the average commission on the small telephone systems he would be selling was approximately $250 per system. I told him if he would see 100 prospects per month, that he would sell four of those prospects a telephone system. Selling four telephone systems would give him $1,000. I hired him on straight commission with no base salary.

He said that sounded great to him because the most he had ever made was $400 per month as a ranch hand and he was ready to make some money. The next morning, I sat him down to cram as much of the telephone "biness" I could into a 22-year-old cowboy with no business experience, no telephone experience and no sales experience. He looked like anything but a professional salesperson in the telecommunications business. In fact, he had none of the qualities I was looking for in an employee, except one: He had an incredible focus on being a success.

At the end of two days of training, Cowboy (that's what I called him then, and still do) went to his cubicle. He took out a sheet of paper and wrote down four things:

1. I will be a success in business.
2. I will see 100 people per month.
3. I will sell four telephone systems per month.
4. I will make $1,000 per month.

He placed this sheet of paper on the cubicle wall in front of him and started to work.

At the end of the first month, he hadn't sold four telephone systems. However, at the end of his first ten days, he had sold *seven* telephone systems.

At the end of his first year, Cowboy hadn't earned $12,000 in commissions. Instead, he had earned over $60,000 in commissions.

He was indeed amazing. One day, he walked into my office with a contract and payment on a telephone system. I asked him how he had sold this one. He said, "I just told her, 'Ma'am, if it don't do nothing but ring and you answer it, it's a heck of a lot prettier than that one you got.' She bought it."

The woman wrote him a check in full for the telephone system, but Cowboy wasn't really sure I would take a check, so he drove her to the bank and had her get cash to pay for the system. He carried thousand-dollar bills into my office and said, "Larry, did I do good?" I assured him that he did good!

After three years, he owned half of my company. At the end of another year, he owned three other companies. At that time we separated as business partners. He was driving a $32,000 black pickup truck. He was wearing $600 cowboy-cut suits, $500 cowboy boots and a three-carat horseshoe-shaped diamond ring. He had become a success in "biness."

What made Cowboy a success? Was it because he was a hard worker? That helped. Was it because he was smarter than everyone else? No. He knew nothing about the telephone business when he started. So what was it? I believe it was because he knew the **Ya Gotta's for Success**:

He was focused on success. He knew that's what he wanted and he went after it.

He took responsibility. He took responsibility for where he was, who he was and what he was (a ranch hand). Then he took *action* to make it different.

He made a decision to leave the ranch in Bartlesville, Oklahoma, and to look for opportunities to become a success.

He changed. There was no way that he could keep doing the things that he had been doing and receive different results. And he was *willing* to do what was necessary to make success happen for him.

He had vision and goals. He saw himself as a success. He also had written down specific goals. He wrote down the four items that he intended to accomplish and put them on the wall in front of him. He saw those goals every day and focused on their accomplishment.

He put action to his goals and stayed with it even when it got tough. It wasn't always easy for him. He experienced slumps like everyone does. He got more doors slammed in his face and telephones in his ear than any salesperson I have ever known. But he never let it stop him. He kept on going.

He asked. Boy, did he ask! First he asked me for a chance, then he asked nearly all the people he came across if they wanted to buy a telephone system from him. And his asking paid off. As he likes to put it,

"Even a blind hog finds an acorn every once in a while." That simply means that if you ask enough, eventually someone will say yes.

He cared. He cared about me and his customers. He discovered that when he cared more about taking care of his customers than he cared about taking care of himself, it wasn't long before he didn't have to worry about taking care of himself.

Most of all, **Cowboy started every day as a winner!** He hit the front door expecting something good to happen. He believed that things were going to go his way regardless of what happened. He had no expectation of failure, only an expectation of success. And I've found that when you expect success and take action on that expectation, you almost always get success.

Cowboy has made millions of dollars. He has also lost it all, only to get it all back again. In his life as in mine, it has been that once you know and practice the principles of success, they will work for you again and again.

He can also be an inspiration to you. He is proof that it's not environment or education or technical skills and ability that make you a success. He proves that it takes more: It takes the principles we so often overlook or take for granted. These are the principles of the **Ya Gotta's for Success**.

Larry Winget

"We're looking for an aggressive, tenacious, salesperson, like, for instance, the one who sold you that suit."

Why Wait? . . . Just Do It!

The big question is whether you are going to be able to say a hearty yes to your adventure.

Joseph Campbell

My father told me that God must surely have a reason for me being the way I am today. I'm beginning to believe it.

I was the kind of kid that things always worked out for. I grew up in Laguna Beach, California, and I loved surfing and sports. But at a time when most kids my age thought only of TV and the beach, I started thinking of ways I could become more independent, see the country and plan my future.

I began working at the age of 10. By the time I was 15, I worked between one to three jobs after school. I made enough money to buy a new motorcycle. I didn't even know how to ride it . But after paying cash for the bike and one year's worth of full insurance coverage, I went to parking lots and learned to ride it. After 15 minutes of figure eights, I rode home. I was 15½, had just received my driver's permit and had bought a new motorcycle. It changed my life.

I wasn't one of those just-for-fun-weekend riders. I loved to ride. Every spare minute of every day, every chance I got, I averaged 100 miles a day on top of that bike. Sunsets and sunrises looked prettier when I enjoyed them from a winding mountain road. Even now, I can close my eyes and still feel the bike naturally beneath me, so naturally that it was a more familiar feeling than walking. As I rode, the cool wind gave me a feeling of total relaxation. While I explored the open road outside, inside I was dreaming about what I wanted my life to be.

Two years and five new motorcycles later, I ran out of roads in California. I read motorcycle magazines every night and one night, a BMW motorcycle ad caught my eye. It showed a muddy motorcycle with a duffel bag on the back parked on the side of a dirt road in front of a large "Welcome to Alaska" sign. One year later, I took a photograph of an even muddier motorcycle in front of that exact same sign. Yes, it was me! At 17 years old I made it to Alaska alone with my bike, conquering over 1,000 miles of dirt highway.

Prior to departing for my seven-week, 17,000-mile camping adventure, my friends said that I was crazy. My parents said that I should wait. Crazy? Wait? For what? Since I was a kid, I had dreamed about going across America on a motorcycle. Something strong inside of me told me that if I didn't go on this trip now, I never would. Besides, when would I have the time? I would be starting college on a scholarship very soon, then a career, perhaps even a family some day. I didn't know if it was just to satisfy me or if in my mind I felt it would somehow transform me from a boy to a man. But what I did know was that for that summer, I was going on the adventure of a lifetime.

I quit all of my jobs and because I was only 17 I had my mother write a letter stating that I had her permission to go on this trip. With $1,400 in my pocket, two duffel bags, a shoe box full of maps strapped to the back of my motorcycle, a pen flashlight for protection and a lot of enthusiasm, I left for Alaska and the East Coast.

I met a lot of people, enjoyed the rugged beauty and lifestyle, ate off the open fire and thanked God every day for giving me this opportunity. Sometimes, I didn't see or hear anyone for two or three days and just rode my motorcycle in endless silence with only the wind racing around my helmet. I didn't cut my hair, I took cold showers at campgrounds when I could, and I even had several unscheduled confrontations with bears during that trip. It was the greatest adventure!

Even though I took several more trips, none can ever compare to that summer. It has always held a special place in my life. I can never go back again and explore the roads and mountains, the forests and glacial waters the same way I did back then on that trip, alone with my motorcycle. I can never make the same trip in the exact same way because at the age of 23, I was in a motorcycle accident on a street in Laguna Beach where I was hit by a drunk driver/drug dealer who left me paralyzed from the ribs down.

At the time of my accident, I was in great shape, both physically and mentally. I was a full-time police officer, still riding my motorcycle on my days off. I was married and financially secure. I had it made. But in the space of less than a second, my whole life changed. I spent eight months in the hospital, got divorced, saw that I could not return to work in the way that I had known it and, along with learning how to deal with chronic pain and a wheelchair, I saw all the dreams I had for my future leaving my reach. Luckily for me, help and support helped new dreams to develop and be fulfilled.

When I think back to all of those trips I took, all of those roads that I traveled, I think of how lucky I was to have been able to do that. Every time I rode, I always said to myself, "Do it now. Enjoy your surroundings, even if you're at a smoggy city intersection; enjoy life because you cannot depend on getting a second chance to be in the same place or do the same things."

After my accident, my father said that God had a reason for me being a paraplegic. I believe it. It has made me a stronger person. I returned to work as a desk officer, bought a home and married again. I also have my own consulting business and am a professional speaker. Every now and again, when things get rough, I remind myself of all the things that I have accomplished, all the things I have yet to accomplish, and my father's words.

Yes, he was right. God sure did have a reason. Most importantly, I remind myself to enjoy every moment of every day. And if you can do something, do it. Do it now!

Glenn McIntyre

7

OVERCOMING OBSTACLES

The marvelous richness of human experience would lose something of rewarding joy if there were no limitations to overcome. The hilltop hour would not be half so wonderful if there were no dark valleys to traverse.

Helen Keller

"HOW ARE WE SUPPOSED TO GET THERE?"

Cartoon by Ted Goff.

Consider This

Effort only fully releases its reward after a person refuses to quit.

Napolean Hill

History has demonstrated that the most notable winners usually encountered heartbreaking obstacles before they triumphed. They won because they refused to become discouraged by their defeats.

B.C. Forbes

Consider this:

- Woody Allen—Academy Award-winning writer, producer and director—flunked motion picture production at New York University and the City College of New York. He also failed English at New York University.
- Leon Uris, author of the bestseller *Exodus*, failed high school English three times.
- When Lucille Ball began studying to be an actress in 1927, she was told by the head instructor of the John Murray Anderson Drama School, "Try any other profession. Any other."
- In 1959, a Universal Pictures executive dismissed Clint Eastwood and Burt Reynolds at the same

meeting with the following statements. To Burt Reynolds: "You have no talent." To Clint Eastwood: "You have a chip on your tooth, your Adam's apple sticks out too far and you talk too slow." As you no doubt know, Burt Reynolds and Clint Eastwood went on to become big stars in the movie industry.

- In 1944, Emmeline Snively, director of the Blue Book Modeling Agency, told modeling hopeful Norma Jean Baker (Marilyn Monroe), "You'd better learn secretarial work or else get married."

- Liv Ullman, who was nominated two times for the Academy Award for Best Actress, failed an audition for the state theater school in Norway. The judges told her she had no talent.

- Malcolm Forbes, the late editor-in-chief of *Forbes* magazine, one of the most successful business publications in the world, failed to make the staff of the school newspaper when he was an under-graduate at Princeton University.

- In 1962, four nervous young musicians played their first record audition for the executives of the Decca Recording Company. The executives were not impressed. While turning down this British rock group called the Beatles, one executive said, "We don't like their sound. Groups of guitars are on the way out."

- Paul Cohen, Nashville "Artists and Repertoire Man" for Decca Records, while firing Buddy Holly from the Decca label in 1956, called Holly "the biggest no-talent I ever worked with." Twenty years later *Rolling Stone* called Holly, along with Chuck Berry, "the major influence on the rock music of the sixties."

- In 1954, Jimmy Denny, manager of the Grand Ole Opry, fired Elvis Presley after one performance.

He told Presley, "You ain't goin' nowhere . . . son. You ought to go back to drivin' a truck." Elvis Presley went on to become the most popular singer in America.

- When Alexander Graham Bell invented the telephone in 1876, it did not ring off the hook with calls from potential backers. After making a demonstration call, President Rutherford Hayes said, "That's an amazing invention, but who would ever want to use one of them?"

- Thomas Edison was probably the greatest inventor in American history. When he first attended school in Port Huron, Michigan, his teachers complained that he was "too slow" and hard to handle. As a result, Edison's mother decided to take her son out of school and teach him at home. The young Edison was fascinated by science. At the age of 10 he had already set up his first chemistry laboratory. Edison's inexhaustible energy and genius (which he reportedly defined as "1 percent inspiration and 99 percent perspiration") eventually produced in his lifetime more than 1,300 inventions.

- When Thomas Edison invented the light bulb, he tried over 2,000 experiments before he got it to work. A young reporter asked him how it felt to fail so many times. He said, "I never failed once. I invented the light bulb. It just happened to be a 2,000-step process."

- In the 1940s, another young inventor named Chester Carlson took his idea to 20 corporations, including some of the biggest in the country. They all turned him down. In 1947— after seven long years of rejections!—he finally got a tiny company in Rochester, New York, the Haloid Company, to purchase the rights to his electrostatic paper-copying process. Haloid became Xerox Corporation, and both it and Carlson became very rich.

- John Milton became blind at age 44. Sixteen years later he wrote the classic *Paradise Lost*.

- When Pablo Casals reached 95, a young reporter threw him the following question. "Mr. Casals, you are 95 and the greatest cellist that ever lived. Why do you still practice six hours a day?" Mr. Casals answered, "Because I think I'm making progress."

- After years of progressive hearing loss, by age 46 German composer Ludwig van Beethoven had become completely deaf. Nevertheless, he wrote his greatest music, including five symphonies, during his later years.

- After having lost both legs in an air crash, British fighter pilot Douglas Bader rejoined the British Royal Air Force with two artificial limbs. During World War II he was captured by the Germans three times—and three times he escaped.

- After having his cancer-ridden leg amputated, young Canadian Terry Fox vowed to run on one leg from coast to coast the entire length of Canada to raise $1 million for cancer research. Forced to quit halfway when the cancer invaded his lungs, he and the foundation he started have raised over $20 million for cancer research.

- Wilma Rudolph was the 20th of 22 children. She was born prematurely and her survival was doubtful. When she was 4 years old, she contracted double pneumonia and scarlet fever, which left her with a paralyzed left leg. At age 9, she removed the metal leg brace she had been dependent on and began to walk without it. By 13 she had developed a rhythmic walk, which doctors said was a miracle. That same year she decided to become a runner. She entered a race and came in last. For the next few years every race she entered, she came in last. Everyone told her to quit, but she kept on running. One day she actually won a race. And then another. From then on she won every race she entered. Eventually this little girl, who was told she would never walk again, went on to win three Olympic gold medals.

My mother taught me very early to believe I could achieve any accomplishment I wanted to. The first was to walk without braces.
Wilma Rudolph

- Franklin D. Roosevelt was paralyzed by polio at the age of 39, and yet he went on to become one of America's most beloved and influential leaders. He was elected president of the United States four times.
- Sarah Bernhardt, who is regarded by many as one of the greatest actresses who ever lived, had her leg amputated as a result of an injury when she was 70 years old, but she continued to act for the next eight years.
- Louis L'Amour, successful author of over 100 western novels with over 200 million copies in print, received 350 rejections before he made his first sale. He later became the first American novelist to receive a special congressional gold medal in recognition of his distinguished career as an author and contributor to the nation through his historically based works.
- In 1953, Julia Child and her two collaborators signed a publishing contract to produce a book tentatively titled *French Cooking for the American Kitchen.* Julia and her colleagues worked on the

book for five years. The publisher rejected the 850-page manuscript. Child and her partners worked for another year totally revising the manuscript. Again the publisher rejected it. But Julia Child did not give up. She and her collaborators went back to work again, found a new publisher and in 1961—eight years after beginning—they published *Mastering the Art of French Cooking,* which has sold more than 1 million copies. In 1966, *Time* magazine featured Julia Child on its cover. Julia Child is still at the top of her field almost 30 years later.

- General Douglas MacArthur might never have gained power and fame without persistence. When he applied for admission to West Point, he was turned down, not once but twice. But he tried a third time, was accepted and marched into the history books.

- Abraham Lincoln entered the Blackhawk War as a captain. By the end of the war, he had been demoted to the rank of private.

- In 1952, Edmund Hillary attempted to climb Mount Everest, the highest mountain then known to humans—29,000 feet straight up. A few weeks after his failed attempt, he was asked to address a group in England. Hillary walked to the edge of the stage, made a fist and pointed at a picture of the mountain. He said in a loud voice, "Mount Everest, you beat me the first time, but I'll beat you the next time because you've grown all you are going to grow . . . but I'm still growing!" On May 29, only one year later, Edmund Hillary succeeded in becoming the first man to climb Mount Everest.

Jack Canfield

Thirty-Nine Years—Too Short—
Too Long—Long Enough

Oh, the worst of all tragedies is not to die young, but to live until I am seventy-five and yet not ever truly to have lived.

Martin Luther King Jr.

From 1929 to 1968 is only 39 short years.
  Too short to gather the fruits of your labor
  Too short to comfort your parents when your
    brother drowns
  Too short to comfort your father when mother dies
  Too short to see your children finish school
  Too short to ever enjoy grandchildren
  Too short to know retirement
Thirty-nine years is just too short.

From 1929 to 1968 is only 39 short years, yet it's
  Too long to be crippled by the manacles of segre-
    gation and the chains of discrimination, it's
  Too long to stand in the quicksand of racial
    injustices, it's
  Too long to receive threatening phone calls, often
    at the rate of forty per day, it's
  Too long to live under the sweltering heat of
    continuous pressure, it's
Too long, 39 years is just too long.

From 1929 to 1968 is only 39 short years, yet it's
Long enough.
It's long enough to journey all the way to India to
learn under a great teacher how to walk
through angry crowds and keep cool.
It's long enough to be chased by police dogs and
lashed by the rushing waters from the fire-
man's hoses because you are dramatizing the
fact that justice has a way of eluding me and
my brother. It's long enough.
It's long enough to spend many days in jail while
protesting the plight of others.
It's long enough to have a bomb thrown into
your home.
It's long enough to teach angry violent men to be
still while you pray for the bombers.
It's long enough.

It's long enough to lead many men to Christianity.
It's long enough to know it's better to go to war
for justice than to live in peace with injustices.
It's long enough to know that more appalling
than bigotry and hatred are those who sit still
and watch injustices each day in silence.
It's long enough to realize that injustices are
undiscriminating and people of all races and
creeds experience its cruel captivity sooner or
later.
It's long enough.

It's long enough to know that when one uses
civil disobedience for his civil rights, he does
not break the laws of the Constitution of the
United States of America—rather he seeks to
uphold the principles all men are created
equal; he seeks to break down local ordinances
that have already broken the laws of the

Constitution of the United States.

It's long enough.

It's long enough to accept invitations to speak to the nation's leaders.

It's long enough to address thousands of people on hundreds of different occasions.

It's long enough to lead 200,000 people to the nation's capital to dramatize that *all* of America's people are heirs to the property of rights to life, liberty and the pursuit of happiness.

It's long enough to enter college at age 15.

It's long enough to finish and earn several degrees.

It's long enough to earn hundreds of awards.

It's long enough to marry and father four children.

It's long enough to become a drum major for peace.

It's long enough to earn a Nobel Peace Prize.

It's long enough to give the $54,000 prize money to the cause of justice.

It's long enough to visit the mountain top. It's certainly long enough to have a dream.

When we note how much Martin Luther King packed into 39 short years, we know it's long enough for any man who loves his country and his fellow man so much that life itself has no value—unless all men can sit at the table of brotherhood as brothers. Thirty-nine years is long enough—for any man to knowingly flirt with death each day of his life—because to spare himself heartaches and sorrow meant two steps backward for his brother tomorrow.

Martin lived for several centuries, all rolled into 39 short years. His memory will live forever.

How wonderful it would be if we could all live
as well.

Martin, like all others, would have welcomed
longevity—yet, when he weighed the facts, he
said, "It's not how long a man lives, but how
well he uses the time allotted him."

And so we salute and honor the memory of a
man who lived in the confusion of injustice for
all his too short, too long, long enough 39
years—

"For He's Free At Last."

Willa Perrier

Nothing but Problems

The man who has no problems is out of the game.

Elbert Hubbard

On Christmas Eve 1993, Norman Vincent Peale, the author of the all-time bestseller *The Power of Positive Thinking,* died at age 95. He was at home surrounded by love, peace and tender care. Norman Vincent Peale deserved nothing less. His positive-thinking ministry had brought peace and renewed confidence to generations of people who realized from his sermons, speeches, radio shows and books that we are responsible for the condition we're in. Since he felt God did not make junk, Norman reminded us that we have two choices every morning when we wake up: we can choose to feel good about ourselves or choose to feel lousy. I can still hear Norman clearly shouting out, "Why would you choose the latter?"

I first met Norman in July 1986. Larry Hughes, who was president of my publishing company, William Morrow & Co., had suggested we think about writing a book together on ethics. We decided to do that, and the next two years working with Norman on *The*

Power of Ethical Management was one of the greatest delights I have ever had in my life.

Ever since that first meeting, Norman had a great impact on my life. He always contended that positive thinkers get positive results because they are not afraid of problems. In fact, rather than thinking of a problem as something that is negative and ought to be removed as quickly as possible, Norman felt problems were a sign of life. To illustrate that point, here is one of his favorite stories, one I have used frequently in my presentations:

> *One day I was walking down the street, when I saw my friend George approaching. It was evident from his downtrodden look that he wasn't overflowing with the ecstasy and exuberance of human existence, which is a high-class way of saying George was dragging bottom.*
>
> *Naturally I asked him, "How are you, George?" While that was meant to be a routine inquiry, George took me very seriously and for 15 minutes he enlightened me on how bad he felt. And the more he talked, the worse I felt.*
>
> *Finally I said to him, "Well, George, I'm sorry to see you in such a depressed state. How did you get this way?" That really set him off.*
>
> *"It's my problems," he said. "Problems—nothing but problems. I'm fed up with problems. If you could get rid of all my problems, I would contribute $5,000 to your favorite charity."*
>
> *Well now, I am never one to turn a deaf ear to such an offer, and so I meditated, ruminated and cogitated on the proposition and came up with an answer that I thought was pretty good.*
>
> *I said, "Yesterday I went to a place where thousands of people reside. As far as I could determine, not one of*

them has any problems. Would you like to go there?"

"When can we leave? That sounds like my kind of place," answered George.

"If that's the case, George," I said, "I'll be happy to take you tomorrow to Woodlawn Cemetery because the only people I know who don't have any problems are dead."

I love that story. It really puts life in perspective. I heard Norman say many times, "If you have no problems at all—I warn you—you're in grave jeopardy— you're on the way out and you don't know it! If you don't believe you have any problems, I suggest that you immediately race from wherever you are, jump into your car and drive home as fast but as safely as possible, run into your house, and go straight to your bedroom and slam the door. Then get on your knees and pray, 'What's the matter, Lord? Don't you trust me anymore? Give me some problems.'"

Ken Blanchard

Angels Never Say "Hello!"

My grandma told me about angels. She said they come knocking at the door of our hearts, trying to deliver a message to us. I saw them in my mind's eye with a big mail sack slung between their wings and a post office cap set jauntily on their head. I wondered if the stamps on their letters said "Heaven Express."

"No use waiting for the angel to open your door," Grandma explained. "You see, there is only one door handle on the door of your heart. Only one bolt. They are on the inside. Your side. You must listen for the angel, throw open the lock and open up that door!"

I loved the story and asked her again and again to tell me, "What does the angel do then?"

"The angel never says 'hello.' You reach out and take the message, and the angel gives you your instructions: 'Arise and go forth!' Then the angel flies away. It is your responsibility to take action."

When I am interviewed by the media, I am often asked how I have built several international businesses without any college education, beginning my business on foot, pushing my two children before me in a dilapidated baby stroller with a wheel that kept coming off.

First I tell the interviewers that I read at least six books a week, and have done so since I was able to read. I hear the voices of all the great achievers in their books.

Next, I explain that every time I hear an angel knock, I just fling open the door. The angel's messages are about new business ideas, books to write and wonderful solutions to problems in my career and personal life. They come very often, in a never-ending flow, a river of ideas.

However, there was one time when the knocking stopped. It happened when my daughter, Lilly, was badly hurt in an accident. She was riding on the back of a forklift her father rented to move some hay for our horses. Lilly and two of the neighbor children begged him to let them ride on the forklift when he took it back to the rental place.

Going down a little hill, the steering gear broke. Her father almost pulled his arms out of their sockets trying to hold the big rig on the road before it turned over. The little neighbor girl broke her arm. Lilly's father was knocked unconscious. Lilly was pinned underneath, with the huge weight of the rig on her left hand. Gasoline spilled on her thigh. Gasoline burns, even if it is not ignited. The neighbor boy was unhurt and kept his wits. He ran out and stopped traffic.

We rushed Lilly to Orthopedic Hospital where they began a long series of operations, each time amputating more of her hand. They told me that when a human limb is cut off, sometimes it can be sewn back on, but not if it is smashed and crushed.

Lilly had just started piano lessons. Because I am a writer, I had looked forward with great anticipation to her taking typing lessons the next year.

During this time I often drove off by myself to cry, not wanting others to see me. I couldn't stop. I found I did not have the concentration to read anything. No angels knocked. There was a heavy silence in my heart. I kept thinking of all the things Lilly would never do because of this terrible accident.

When we took her back to the hospital for the eighth amputation, my spirit was very low. I kept thinking over and over, "She will never type! Never type. Never type."

We set her bag down in the hospital room and suddenly turned around because a young teenage girl in the next bed said to us in a commanding voice: "I've been waiting for you! You go down the hall right now, third room on the left! There is a boy there who was hurt in a motorcycle accident. You go down there and lift up his spirit, right now!"

She had the voice of a field marshal. We immediately obeyed her. We talked to the boy and encouraged him, and then came back to Lilly's hospital room.

For the first time I noticed that this unusual girl was bent way over. "Who are you?" I asked.

"My name is Tony Daniels," she grinned. "I go to the handicapped high school. This time the doctors are going to make me a whole inch taller! You see, I had polio. I have had many operations."

She had the charisma and strength of a General Schwartzkopf. I couldn't help the words that came flying out of my mouth. I gasped, "But you aren't handicapped!"

"Oh, yes, you are right," she replied, looking sideways at me. "They teach us down at our school that we are never handicapped as long as we can help someone else. Now, if you met my schoolmate who teaches the typing class, you might think she is handicapped because she was born with no arms and no legs. But she helps all of us by teaching us typing, with a wand between her teeth."

Ka bang! Suddenly I heard it—the clanging noise of pounding and kicking and yelling at the door of my heart!

I ran out of the room and down the corridor to find a pay phone. I called IBM and asked for the office manager. I told him my little girl had lost nearly all of her left hand, and asked him if they had one-hand touch-typing charts.

He replied, "Yes, we do! We have charts for the right hand, the left hand, charts that show how to use your feet with pedals, and even to type with a wand between your teeth. The charts are free. Where would you like me to send them?"

When we were finally able to take Lilly back to school, I took the one-hand typing charts with me. Her hand and arm were still in a cast with big bandages around it. I asked the school principal if Lilly could take typing, even though she was too young, instead of gym. He told me it had never been done before, and that perhaps the typing teacher would not want to go to the extra trouble, but I could ask him if I wanted to.

When I stepped into the typing class I noticed immediately that all around the room were signs with quotations from Florence Nightingale, Ben Franklin, Ralph Waldo Emerson and Winston Churchill. I took a deep breath, realizing I was in the right place. The teacher said he had never taught one-hand typing before but that he would work with Lilly every lunch period. "We will learn one-hand touch-typing together."

Soon Lilly touch-typed all of her homework for her English class. Her English teacher that year was a polio victim. His right arm hung helplessly by his side. He scolded her, "Your mother is babying you, Lilly. You have a good right hand. You do your own homework."

"Oh, no sir." She smiled at him. "I'm up to 50 words a minute one-handed in my touch-typing. I have the one-hand IBM charts!"

The English teacher sat down suddenly. Then he said slowly, "Being able to type has always been my dream."

"Come on over during lunch time. The back of my charts have the other hand. I'll teach you!" Lilly told him.

It was after the first lunch-time lesson that she came home and said, "Mama, Tony Daniels was right. I'm not handicapped anymore, because I am helping someone else fulfill his dream."

Today, Lilly is the author of two internationally acclaimed books. She has taught all of our office staff to use our Apple computers with our mouse pad on the left side, because that is where she makes hers fly around with her remaining finger and the stump of her thumb.

Shush. Listen! Do you hear the knocking? Throw the bolt! Open the door! Please think of me and remember: Angels never say "hello." Their greeting is always "Arise and go forth!"

Dottie Walters

Why Do These Things Have to Happen?

We are all pencils in the hand of God.

Mother Teresa

One of my joys and passions is my voice. I love to perform in our local community theaters. My throat became very sore during a particularly grueling show run. It was my first time performing an operatic piece, and I was terrified I had actually done damage to my vocal cords. I was a lead and we were about to open. So I made an appointment with my family doctor where I waited for an hour. I finally left in a huff, went back to work, grabbed a phone book and found a throat specialist close by. Once more I made an appointment and off I went.

The nurse showed me in and I sat down to wait for the doctor. I was feeling very disgruntled. I rarely get sick and here I was sick when I needed to be healthy. Besides, I had to take time out of my work-day to go to two different doctors, both of whom kept me waiting. It was very frustrating. Why do these things have to happen? A moment later the nurse came back in and said, "May I ask you something personal?"

This seemed odd; what else do they ask you but personal questions in a doctor's office? But I looked at the nurse and replied, "Yes, of course."

"I noticed your hand," she said a bit hesitantly.

I lost half of my left hand in a forklift accident when I was 11. I think it is one of the reasons I didn't follow my dream of performing in theater, although everyone says, "Gee, I never noticed! You are so natural." In the back of my mind I thought that they only wanted to see perfect people on stage. No one would want to see me. Besides, I'm too tall, overweight, not really talented . . . no, they don't want to see me. But I love musical comedies and I do have a good voice. So one day I tried out at our local community theater. I was the first one they cast! That was three years ago. Since then, I have been cast in almost everything I tried out for.

The nurse continued, "What I need to know is how it has affected your life."

Never in the 25 years since it happened has someone asked me this. Maybe they'll say, "Does it bother you?" but never anything as sweeping as, "How has it affected your life?"

After an awkward pause, she said, "You see I just had a baby, and her hand is like yours. I, well, I need to know how it has affected your life."

"How has it affected my life?" I thought about it a bit so I could think of the right words to say. Finally, I said, "It has affected my life, but not in a bad way— I do many things that people with two normal hands find difficult. I type about 75 words a minute, I play guitar, I have ridden and shown horses for years, I even have a Horsemaster Degree. I'm involved in musical theater and I am a professional speaker, I'm constantly in front of a crowd. I do television shows four or five times a year. I think it was never 'difficult' because of the love and encouragement of my family.

They always talked about all the great notoriety I would get because I would learn how to do things with one hand that most people had trouble doing with two. We were all very excited about that. That was the main focus, not the handicap.

"Your daughter does not have a problem. She is normal. You are the one who will teach her to think of herself as anything else. She will come to know she is 'different,' but you will teach her that *different* is wonderful. Normal means you are average. What's fun about that?"

She was silent for a while. Then she simply said, "Thank you" and walked out.

I sat there thinking, "Why do these things have to happen?" Everything happens for a reason—even that forklift falling on my hand. All the circumstances leading up to me being at this doctor's office and this moment in time happened for a reason.

The doctor came in, looked at my throat and said he wanted to anesthetize and put a probe down it to examine it. Well, singers are very paranoid about putting medical instruments down their throats, especially ones so rough they need to be anesthetized! I said, "No thanks," and walked out.

The next day, my throat was completely better.

Why do these things have to happen?

Lilly Walters

The Finest Steel Gets Sent
Through the Hottest Furnace

*Character cannot be developed in ease
and quiet. Only through experiences of trial
and suffering can the soul be strengthened,
vision cleared, ambition inspired and success achieved.*

Helen Keller

I'll never forget the night in 1946 when disaster and
challenge visited our home.

My brother George came home from football practice and collapsed with a 104-degree temperature.
After an examination, the doctor informed us it was
polio. This was before the days of Dr. Salk; polio was
well-known in Webster, Missouri, having killed and
crippled many children and teenagers.

After the crisis had passed, the doctor felt it was his
duty to inform George of the horrible truth. "I hate to
tell you this, son," he said, "but the polio has taken
such a toll that you'll probably never walk again without a limp, and your left arm will be useless."

George had always envisioned himself as a championship wrestler his senior year, after just missing
the championship the season before. Barely able to

speak, George whispered, "Doctor ..."

"Yes," said the doctor leaning over the bed, "what is it, my boy?"

"Go to hell," said George in a voice filled with determination.

The next day the nurse walked into his room to find him lying flat on his face on the floor.

"What's going on?" asked the shocked nurse.

"I'm walking," George calmly replied.

He refused the use of any braces or even a crutch. Sometimes it would take him 20 minutes to get out of the chair, but he refused any offers of aid.

I remember seeing him lift a tennis ball with as much effort as a healthy man would lift a 100-pound barbell.

I also remember seeing him step out on the mat as captain of the wrestling team.

But the story doesn't stop there. The following year, after being named to start for Missouri Valley College in one of the first football games to be televised locally, he came down with mononucleosis.

It was my brother Bob who helped reinforce George's already strong philosophy of never giving up.

The family was sitting in his room at the hospital when Valley's quarterback completed a 12-yard pass to the tight end and the announcer said, "And George Schlatter makes the first catch of the game."

Shocked, we all looked at the bed to make sure George was still there. Then we realized what had happened. Bob, who had also made the starting lineup, had worn George's number so George could spend the afternoon hearing himself catching six passes and making countless tackles.

As he overcame mono, he did it with the lesson Bob taught him that day—there is always a way!

George was destined to spend the next three falls in the hospital. In 1948, it was after he stepped on a rusty nail. In 1949, it was tonsillitis, just before he was to sing in an audition for Phil Harris. And in 1950, it was third-degree burns over 40 percent of his body and collapsed lungs. His life had been saved by my brother Alan who, after an explosion had set George's body on fire, put the flames out by throwing himself on George. He received serious burns himself.

But after each challenge, George came back stronger and more sure of his own ability to overcome any obstacle. He had read that if one looks at the roadblocks, he isn't looking at the goal.

Armed with these gifts of the spirit and the laughter of the soul, he entered the world of show business and revolutionized television by creating and producing such innovative shows as "Laugh In" and "American Comedy Awards," and has won an Emmy for his special on Sammy Davis Jr.

He had literally been through the furnace and had come out of it with a soul as strong as steel, and used it to strengthen and entertain a nation.

John Wayne Schlatter

The Race

I

"Quit! Give up! You're beaten!"
  They shout at me and plead.
"There's just too much against you now;
  This time you can't succeed!"

And as I start to hang my head
  In front of failure's face,
My downward fall is broken by
  The memory of a race.

And hope refills my weakened will
  As I recall that scene;
For just the thought of that short race
  Rejuvenates my being.

II

A children's race—young boys, young men—
  How I remember well.
Excitement, sure! But also fear;
  It wasn't hard to tell.

They all lined up so full of hope
  Each thought to win that race.
Or tie for first, or if not that,
  At least take second place.

And fathers watched from off the side
  Each cheering for his son.
And each boy hoped to show his dad
  That he would be the one.

The whistle blew and off they went!
  Young hearts and hopes afire.
To win and be the hero there
  Was each young boy's desire.

And one boy in particular
  Whose dad was in the crowd
Was running near the lead and thought:
  "My dad will be so proud!"

But as he speeded down the field
  Across a shallow dip,
The little boy who thought to win
  Lost his step and slipped.

Trying hard to catch himself
  His hands flew out to brace,
And mid the laughter of the crowd
  He fell flat on his face.

So down he fell and with him hope
  —He couldn't win it now—
Embarrassed, sad, he only wished
  To disappear somehow.

But as he fell his dad stood up
  And showed his anxious face,
Which to the boy so clearly said:
  "Get up and win the race!"

He quickly rose, no damage done
  —Behind a bit, that's all—
And ran with all his mind and might
  To make up for his fall.

So anxious to restore himself
　　—To catch up and to win—
His mind went faster than his legs;
　　He slipped and fell again!

He wished then he had quit before
　　With only one disgrace.
"I'm hopeless as a runner now;
　　I shouldn't try to race."

But in the laughing crowd he searched
　　And found his father's face;
That steady look which said again:
　　"Get up and win the race!"

So he jumped up to try again
　　—Ten yards behind the last—
"If I'm to gain those yards," he thought,
　　"I've got to move real fast."

Exerting everything he had
　　He gained eight or ten,
But trying so hard to catch the lead
　　He slipped and fell again!

Defeat! He lied there silently
　　—A tear dropped from his eye—
"There's no sense running anymore:
　　Three strikes: I'm out! Why try?"

The will to rise had disappeared;
　　All hope had fled away;
So far behind, so error-prone:
　　A loser all the way.

"I've lost, so what's the use," he thought
　　"I'll live with my disgrace."
But then he thought about his dad
　　Who soon he'd have to face.

"Get up," an echo sounded low.
  "Get up and take your place;
You were not meant for failure here.
  Get up and win the race."

"With borrowed will get up," it said,
  "You haven't lost at all.
For winning is no more than this:
  To rise each time you fall."

So up he rose to run once more,
  And with a new commit
He resolved that win or lose
  At least he wouldn't quit.

So far behind the others now,
  —The most he'd ever been—
Still he gave it all he had
  And ran as though to win.

Three times he'd fallen, stumbling;
  Three times he rose again:
Too far behind to hope to win
  He still ran to the end.

They cheered the winning runner
  As he crossed the line first place.
Head high, and proud, and happy;
  No falling, no disgrace.

But when the fallen youngster
  Crossed the line last place,
The crowd gave him the greater cheer,
  For finishing the race.

And even though he came in last
  With head bowed low, unproud,
You would have thought he'd won the race
  To listen to the crowd.

And to his dad he sadly said,
  "I didn't do too well."
"To me, you won," his father said.
  "You rose each time you fell."

III

And when things seem dark and hard
  And difficult to face,
The memory of that little boy
  Helps me in my race.

For all of life is like that race.
  With ups and downs and all.
And all you have to do to win,
  Is rise each time you fall.

"Quit! Give up, you're beaten!"
  They still shout in my face.
But another voice within me says:
  "GET UP AND WIN THE RACE!"

D.H. Groberg

Cartoon by Ted Goff.

After a While

After a while you learn the subtle difference
  between holding a hand and chaining a soul
And you learn that love doesn't mean leaning
  and company doesn't always mean security
And you begin to learn that kisses aren't contracts
  and presents aren't promises
And you begin to accept your defeats
  with your head up and your eyes ahead with the
  grace of a woman, not the grief of a child
And you learn to build all your roads on today
  because tomorrow's ground is too uncertain for
  plans.
After a while you learn that even sunshine burns
  if you get too much.
So you plant your own garden and decorate your
  own soul instead of waiting for someone to bring
  you flowers.
And you learn that you really can endure
that you really are strong
and you really do have worth
And you learn and you learn
  with every
  goodbye you learn . . .

Veronica A. Shoffstall
Submitted by Barbara Cowdy

Reprinted by permission of Veronica A. Shoffstall. ©1971 Veronica A. Shoffstall.

Summit America

"Why me?" Todd screamed as his dad pulled his bloody body out of the murky lake and into the boat. Todd remained conscious as his father, two brothers and three friends sped to shore to get help.

It was all too surreal. Everyone had just spent a fun-filled day of water-skiing at the lake in Oklahoma where his grandparents lived. Todd wanted to go inner-tubing after everyone finished water-skiing. As he was untangling the ski ropes, the gears kicked into reverse and sucked his legs into the propellers, all in a flash of a moment. No one heard him scream until it was too late! Now he was in the hospital, hanging onto his life.

Both legs were severely injured. The sciatic nerve in his right leg had been severed, causing his leg to be permanently paralyzed from the knee down to his toes. The doctors said there was a chance he would never walk again. Todd slowly recovered from his wounds, but bone disease eventually set into his right foot. For the next seven years, he physically and emotionally battled to keep his leg. However, the time had finally come for him to face his biggest fear.

On a grim day in April, 1981, Todd lay conscious on the operating table at Massachusetts General waiting for the procedure to take place. He spoke calmly to the hospital staff about what kind of pizza he wanted to eat after the surgery. "I'd like Canadian bacon and pineapple," he joked. As the dreaded moment approached, a wave of calmness swept over him. Peace filled his heart as he thought of a Bible verse from his childhood, "Righteousness goes before him and prepares the way for his steps."

Todd knew with an unwavering conviction that his next step was to go through with the amputation. Any lingering doubt had vanished, and courage to face the inevitable prevailed. To obtain the lifestyle he desired, he had to lose his leg. In a few short minutes the leg was gone, but his whole future opened up.

He studied psychology at the suggestion of friends and family. He graduated *magna cum laude*, then took a job as clinical director of the Amputee Resource Center in Southern California. With his background in psychology and his personal experience as an amputee, he began to notice how he was able to inspire other amputees through his work.

"The steps I must take in my life are ordered," he remembered. "I guess I'm on the right path, but what is my next step?" he wondered.

Until the accident he led a normal life. He hiked, camped, played sports, flirted with girls and hung out with his buddies. After his injury, he continued to socialize with his friends, but he had trouble playing sports. The artificial leg he received after the amputation allowed him to walk again, but not much more.

There were nights Todd would dream of running through grassy fields, only to wake up to the harsh reality of his situation. He desperately wanted to run again.

In 1993, he got his wish. A new type of prosthesis, called a Flex-Foot, was developed. He acquired one through his prosthetist.

At first, he struggled to run, tripping over his feet

and gasping for breath. However, with perseverance he was soon able to run 12 miles a day.

As he developed his abilities, a friend stumbled across an article in a magazine he thought Todd would find interesting. An organization was looking for an amputee to climb the highest mountain in each of the 50 states. There would be four other disabled climbers, and they would attempt to break a record by climbing all 50 highpoints in 100 days or less.

The idea excited Todd. "Why not go for it?" he thought. "I used to love to hike and now I have an opportunity to explore my limits." He applied for the position and was immediately accepted.

The expedition was set to begin in April 1994. Todd had almost a year to get prepared. He began to train for the climb by working out daily, changing his diet and practicing rock climbing on weekends. Everyone agreed it was a good idea, but some thought it might not be the most responsible choice.

Todd didn't let those with negative concerns hold him back. He knew this was the right thing to do. When he prayed for direction, he was clear that this was to be the next step in his life.

Everything was working out perfectly—until February 1994, when he received some discouraging news. The funding for the expedition fell through. The project coordinator said he was sorry, but there was nothing left to do but disband the project.

"I will not quit!" Todd exclaimed. "I have put too much time and work into this to give up now. There is a message here that must be heard and, God willing, I'll find a way to make this expedition happen!"

Undaunted by the news, Todd set out to put the wheels in motion. During the next six weeks, he gathered enough financial support to get a new expedition under way. He garnered the support of a few friends to help him with the logistics of the climb. Whit Rambach would be his climbing partner, and I, Lisa Manley, would handle business from the home front. With everything now in order, he took off as scheduled with his new expedition called "Summit America."

As Todd prepared for the expedition, he learned that only 31 people had ever reached the summit of all 50 highpoints. More people have successfully climbed Mt. Everest, the highest mountain in the world.

Todd and Whit began the record for climbing all 50 highpoints at 5:10 P.M. on June 1, 1994 on Mt. McKinley in Alaska. The previous record holder, Adrian Crane, and a military sergeant, Mike Vining, assisted them in their climb on Denali, the Indian name for Mt. McKinley.

"The conditions on the mountain were extremely unpredictable," said Todd. "Storms could blow in within hours. It's like a game of cat and mouse trying to make it to the top.

"The weather got to minus 30 degrees Fahrenheit at times," he said. "It took us 12 days to battle the weather, altitude sickness and the reality of the danger. I knew the mountain could be dangerous, but I didn't realize just how dangerous until two frozen bodies were being dragged down the mountain in front of me.

"It was one step at a time. The last thousand feet were the most difficult. I was taking three breaths for every step. I kept telling myself that my message would only be heard if I made it to the top. This realization propelled me to the summit."

The rest of the expedition was fast-paced and exciting. Hooked on Phonics came to Summit America's rescue by financing the rest of the climb. People took an interest in Todd, his determination to break the record, and his story. His message was being told in newspapers and on television and radio as he traveled around the country.

Everything was right on track until it was time to climb the 47th highpoint, Mt. Hood in Oregon. One week earlier, two people lost their lives on that mountain. Everyone advised Todd and Whit not to make the climb. They said it wasn't worth the risk.

Full of uncertainty and apprehension, Todd contacted his old high-school friend and expert mountaineer, Fred Zalokar. When Fred heard his predicament, he said, "Todd, you've come too far to quit now. Fly me into town and I'm going take you up that mountain—safely."

After a number of discussions with mountain authorities and hours of careful planning, Todd, Whit and Fred successfully made it to the summit of Mt. Hood. Now only three more highpoints stood between Todd and the record.

Then on August 7, 1994, at 11:57 A.M., Todd stood victorious at the peak of Hawaii's Mauna Kea. He had climbed all 50 highpoints in just 66 days, 21 hours and 47 minutes, shattering the old climbing record by 35 days!

Even more remarkable, Todd was an amputee who shattered a record set by a man with two good legs.

Todd was elated, not only because he had set a new world climbing record, but because he now knew the answer to the question, "Why me?" that had haunted him ever since his accident at the lake.

At age 33, he saw how this triumph over his tragedy could be used to encourage people everywhere to believe that they could make it through their personal challenges.

Throughout the climb and to this day, Todd Huston is bringing his message to people everywhere. With a calm assurance he states, "Through faith in God and a belief in the abilities God gives you, you can overcome whatever challenges you face in life."

Lisa Manley

An Undiscovered Masterpiece

Nothing in the world can take the place of perseverance. Talent will not; nothing is more common than unsuccessful men with talent. Genius will not; unrewarded genius is almost a proverb. Persistence and determination alone are omnipotent.

Calvin Coolidge

A few years ago, my friend Sue had some fairly serious health problems. She had been an invalid as a child and still suffered from a birth defect that had left a hole in one of the chambers of her heart. The births of her five children, beginning with a difficult C-section, had also taken their toll. She had suffered surgery after surgery and had also put on weight for several years. Diets had not helped her. She suffered almost constantly from undiagnosed pain. Her husband, Dennis, had learned to accept her limitations. He constantly hoped her health would improve, but he did not really believe it ever would.

One day they sat down as a family and drew up a "wish list" of the things they wanted most out of life. One of Sue's items was to run in a marathon. Given her history and physical limitations, Dennis thought her goal was completely unrealistic, but Sue became committed to it.

She began by running very slowly in the subdivision where they lived. Every day she ran just a little farther than she had the day before—just one driveway more. "When will I ever be able to run a mile?" Sue asked one day. Soon she was running three. Then five. I'll let Dennis tell the rest of the story in his own words:

I remember Sue telling me something she had learned: "The subconscious and the nervous system cannot tell the difference between real and vividly imagined situations." We can change ourselves for the better and cause ourselves to subconsciously pursue our most precious desires with almost total success, if we crystallize the images clearly enough in our minds. I knew Sue believed it—she had registered to run in the St. George Marathon in southern Utah.

"Can the mind believe an image that will lead to self-destruction?" I asked myself as I drove the mountainous road from Cedar City to St. George, Utah. I parked our van near the finish line and waited for Sue to come in. The rain was steady and the wind was cold. The marathon had started over five hours ago. Several cold and injured runners had been transported past me, and I began to panic. The image of Sue alone and cold, off the road somewhere, made me sick with worry. The fast and strong competitors had finished long ago, and runners were becoming more and more sparse. Now I could not see anyone in either direction.

Almost all of the cars along the marathon route had left, and some normal traffic was beginning. I was able to drive directly up the race route. There were still no runners in view after driving almost two miles. Then I went around a bend in the road and spotted a small group running up ahead. As I approached, I could see Sue in the company of three others. They were smiling and talking as they ran. They were on the opposite side of the road as I pulled off and called between the now-steady traffic, "Are you okay?"

"Oh, yes!" Sue said, panting only mildly. Her new friends smiled at me.

"How far to the finish line?" one of them asked.

"Only a couple of miles," I said.

A couple of miles? I thought. *Am I crazy?* I noticed that two of the runners were limping. I could hear their feet sloshing in wet sneakers. I wanted to say to them that they had run a good race and offer them a ride in, but I could see the resolve in their eyes. I turned the van around and followed from a distance, watching for one or all of them to fall. They had been running for over five and a half hours! I sped around them and up to within a mile of the finish and waited.

As Sue came into view again, I could see her begin to struggle. Her pace slowed and she grimaced. She looked at her legs in horror as if they did not want to work any longer. Somehow, she kept moving, almost staggering.

The small group was becoming more spread out. Only a woman in her twenties was near Sue. It was obvious that they had become friends during the race. I was caught up in the scene and began running along with them. After a hundred yards or so I tried to speak, to offer some great words of wisdom and motivation, but my words and my breath failed.

The finish line came into sight. I was grateful it had not been completely dismantled, because I felt that the real winners were just now coming in. One of the runners, a slim teenager, stopped running, sat down, and started to cry. I watched as some people, probably his family, came and carried him to their car. I could also see that Sue was in agony—but she had dreamed about this day for two years and she would not be denied. She knew she would finish, and this knowledge allowed her to confidently—even happily—pick up her pace the last hundred yards to the finish line.

Few people were left to congratulate my wife and marathon runner extraordinaire. She had run a smart race, stopping to stretch regularly, drinking plenty of water at the various water stops, and pacing herself well. She had been the leader of a small group of less-experienced runners. She had inspired and encouraged most of them home with her words of confidence and assurance. They openly praised and embraced her as we rejoiced in the park.

"She made us believe we could do it," her new friend stated.

"She described so vividly how it would be to finish that I knew I could do it," another said.

The rain had quit, and we walked and talked in the park. I looked at Sue. She was carrying herself differently. Her head was more erect. Her shoulders were squared. Her walk, even though she was limping, had a new confidence. Her voice held a new, quiet dignity. It was not as if she had become someone new; it was more as if she had discovered a real self she had not known before. The painting was not yet dry, but I knew she was an undiscovered masterpiece with a million things left to learn about herself. She truly liked her newly discovered self. So did I.

Charles A. Coonradt

If I Could Do It, You Can Too!

I began life, literally, with nothing. Given up as an infant by my biological mother, an unmarried young woman from the small town of Moose Jaw in Saskatchewan, Canada, I was adopted by a poor, middle-aged couple, John and Mary Linkletter.

My adoptive father was one of the warmest men I've ever known, but he had absolutely no ability as a businessman. A part-time evangelical preacher, he also tried selling insurance, running a small general store and making shoes, all rather unsuccessfully. Eventually we found ourselves living in a charity home run by a local church in San Diego. Then Dad Linkletter felt called by God to become a full-time preacher, and we had even less money. And what we did have was usually shared with whatever neighborhood derelict happened to be looking for a meal.

I graduated from high school early and hit the road as a hobo at the tender age of 16 with the idea of finding my fortune. One of the first things I found, however, was the wrong end of a pistol: my traveling companion and I were held up by a couple of toughs who found us sleeping in a boxcar.

"Put your hands straight out and lie flat!" one of the men ordered. "If this match goes out and I hear anything more I'll shoot." As they searched our pockets and felt around our middles, I wondered if money was all they wanted. I was frightened because I had heard stories of older hobos sexually attacking young boys. Just then, the match went out . . . and was hastily relit. We did not move! The thieves found $1.30 on me but missed $10.00 I had sewn into my coat lining. They also took two dollars from my friend, Denver Fox.

The match went out again and I could tell by their hesitation that they were undecided about something. As Denver and I lay there, inches apart in the darkness, I heard the hammer of the pistol click back and a cold chill ran down my back. I knew they were considering killing us. There was little risk for them. The rain hammering down on the outside of the box-car would drown out any noise. Frozen with terror, I thought of my father and how he would have prayed for me had he known. Suddenly fear left me, and peace and calm returned. As if in response to my own restored self-assurance, they moved back toward us. Then I could feel one of the men push something against my arm.

"Here's your thirty cents," he said. "Breakfast money."

Today I can look back on 45 years as a star of two of the longest-running shows in broadcasting history; I can reflect on the success I've had as a businessman, author, and lecturer; and I can be proud of my wonderful family life—58 years with the same wife, five children, seven grandchildren, and eight great-grandchildren. I mention this not to be boastful but to encourage others who are at the lower rung of the economic ladder. Keep in mind where I started and remember, if I could do it, you can, too! Yes—you can!

Art Linkletter

What Happened?

A young man played, or I should say practiced, football at an Ivy League university. "Jerry" wasn't skilled enough to play more than occasionally in the regular season games, but in four years this dedicated, loyal young man never missed a practice.

The coach, deeply impressed with Jerry's loyalty and dedication to the team, also marveled at his evident devotion to his father. Several times the coach had seen Jerry and his visiting father laughing and talking as they walked arm-in-arm around the campus. But the coach had never met the father or talked with Jerry about him.

During Jerry's senior year and a few nights before the most important game of the season—a traditional rivalry that matched Army-Navy, Georgia-Georgia Tech or Michigan-Ohio State in intensity—the coach heard a knock on his door. Opening it, he saw the young man, his face full of sadness.

"Coach, my father just died," Jerry murmured. "Is it all right if I miss practice for a few days and go home?"

The coach said he was very sorry to hear the news and, of course, it was all right for him to go home. As Jerry murmured a "thank you" and turned to leave, the coach added, "Please don't feel you have to return in time for next Saturday's game. You certainly are excused from that, too." The youth nodded and left.

But on Friday night, just hours before the big game, Jerry again stood in the coach's doorway. "Coach, I'm back," he said, "and I have a request. May I please start the game tomorrow?"

The coach tried to dissuade the youth from his plea in light of the importance of the game to the team. But finally he consented.

That night the coach tossed and turned. Why had he said yes to the youth? The opposing team was favored to win by three touchdowns. He needed his best players in for the entire game. Suppose the opening kickoff came to Jerry and he fumbled. Suppose he started the game and they lost by five or six touchdowns.

Obviously he could not let the youth play. It was out of the question. But he had promised.

So, as the bands played and the crowd roared, Jerry stood at the goal line awaiting the opening kickoff. *The ball probably won't go to him anyway*, the coach thought to himself. Then the coach would run one series of plays, making sure the other halfback and the fullback carried the ball, and take the youth out of the game. That way he wouldn't have to worry about a crucial fumble, and he would have kept his promise.

"Oh no!" the coach groaned as the opening kickoff floated end over end right into Jerry's arms. But instead of fumbling, as the coach expected, Jerry hugged the ball tightly, dodged three onrushing defenders and raced to midfield before he was finally tackled.

The coach had never seen Jerry run with such agility and power, and perhaps sensing something, he had the quarterback call Jerry's signal. The quarterback handed off, and Jerry responded by breaking tackles for a 20-yard gain. A few plays later he carried the ball over the goal line.

The favored opponents were stunned. Who was this kid? He wasn't even in their scouting reports, for until then he had played a total of three minutes all year.

The coach left Jerry in, and he played the entire first half on both offense and defense. Tackling, intercepting and knocking down passes, blocking, running—he did it all.

At halftime the underdogs led by two touchdowns. During the second half Jerry continued to inspire the team. When the final gun sounded, his team had won.

In the locker-room bedlam reserved only for teams that have fought the impossible fight and triumphed, the coach sought out Jerry and found him sitting quietly, head in hands, in a far corner.

"Son, what happened out there?" the coach asked as he put his arm around him. "You can't play as well as you did. You're just not that fast, not that strong nor that skilled. What happened?"

Jerry looked up at the coach and said softly, "You see, Coach, my father was blind. This is the first game he ever saw me play."

Author Unknown
Submitted by Chuck Dodge

Let There Be Peace

A wise old gentleman retired and purchased a modest home near a junior high school. He spent the first few weeks of his retirement in peace and contentment . . . then a new school year began. The very next afternoon three young boys, full of youthful, after-school enthusiasm, came down his street, beating merrily on every trash can they encountered. The crashing percussion continued day after day, until finally the wise old man decided it was time to take some action.

The next afternoon, he walked out to meet the young percussionists as they banged their way down the street. Stopping them, he said, "You kids are a lot of fun. I like to see you express your exuberance like that. Used to do the same thing when I was your age. Will you do me a favor? I'll give you each a dollar if you'll promise to come around every day and do your thing."

The kids were elated and continued to do a bang-up job on the trash cans. After a few days, the old-timer greeted the kids again, but this time he had a sad smile on his face. "This recession's really putting a big dent in my income," he told them. "From now on, I'll only be able to pay you 50 cents to beat on the cans." The noisemakers were obviously displeased, but they did accept his offer and continued their afternoon ruckus.

A few days later, the wily retiree approached them again as they drummed their way down the street. "Look," he said, "I haven't received my Social Security check yet, so I'm not going to be able to give you more than 25 cents. Will that be okay?"

"A lousy quarter?" the drum leader exclaimed. "If you think we're going to waste our time, beating these cans around for a quarter, you're nuts! No way, mister. We quit!" And the old man enjoyed peace and serenity for the rest of his days.

Gentle Spaces News

8

ECLECTIC WISDOM

Life is a succession of lessons which must be lived to be understood.

Helen Keller

"You mean I do the Hokie Pokie and I turn myself around, and that's what it's all about?"

Wisdom

Three cowboys had been riding the range since early in the morning. One of them was a member of the Navajo Nation. Being busy with herding stray cattle all day, there had been no time for the three of them to eat. Toward the end of the day, two of the cowboys started talking about how hungry they were and about the huge meals they were going to eat when they reached town. When one of the cowboys asked the Navajo if he was also hungry, he just shrugged his shoulders and said, "No."

Later that evening, after they had arrived in town, all three ordered large steak dinners. As the Navajo proceeded to eat everything in sight with great gusto, one of his friends reminded him that less than an hour earlier he had told them that he was not hungry. "Not wise to be hungry then," he replied. "No food."

Author Unknown

Napoleon and the Furrier

Do not look back in anger, or forward in fear, but around in awareness.

James Thurber

During Napoleon's invasion of Russia, his troops were battling in the middle of yet another small town in that endless wintry land, when he was accidentally separated from his men. A group of Russian Cossacks spotted him and began chasing him through the twisting streets. Napoleon ran for his life and ducked into a little furrier's shop on a side alley. As Napoleon entered the shop, gasping for breath, he saw the furrier and cried piteously, "Save me, save me! Where can I hide?" The furrier said, "Quick, under this big pile of furs in the corner," and he covered Napoleon up with many furs.

No sooner had he finished than the Russian Cossacks burst in the door, shouting "Where is he? We saw him come in." Despite the furrier's protests, they tore his shop apart trying to find Napoleon. They poked into the pile of furs with their swords but didn't find him. Soon, they gave up and left.

After some time, Napoleon crept out from under the furs, unharmed, just as Napoleon's personal guards came in the door. The furrier turned to Napoleon and said timidly, "Excuse me for asking this question of such a great man, but what was it like to be under those furs, knowing that the next moment would surely be your last?"

Napoleon drew himself up to his full height and said to the furrier indignantly, "How could you ask such a question of me, the Emperor Napoleon! Guards, take this impudent man out, blindfold him and execute him. I, myself, will personally give the command to fire!"

The guards grabbed the poor furrier, dragged him outside, stood him up against a wall and blindfolded him. The furrier could see nothing, but he could hear the movements of the guards as they slowly shuffled into a line and prepared their rifles, and he could hear the soft ruffling sound of his clothing in the cold wind. He could feel the wind tugging gently at his clothes and chilling his cheeks, and the uncontrollable trembling in his legs. Then he heard Napoleon clear his throat and call out slowly, "Ready... aim ... " In that moment, knowing that even these few sensations were about to be taken from him forever, a feeling that he couldn't describe welled up in him as tears poured down his cheeks.

After a long period of silence, the furrier heard footsteps approaching him and the blindfold was stripped from his eyes. Still partially blinded by the sudden sunlight, he saw Napoleon's eyes looking deeply and intently into his own—eyes that seemed to see into every dusty corner of his being. Then Napoleon said softly, "Now you know."

Steve Andreas

Footprints

One night I dreamed a dream.
I was walking along the beach with my Lord.
Across the dark sky flashed scenes from my life.
For each scene, I noticed two sets
of footprints in the sand,
one belonging to me
and one to my Lord.
When the last scene of my life shot before me
I looked back at the footprints in the sand.
There was only one set of footprints.
I realized that this was at the lowest
and saddest times of my life.
This always bothered me
and I questioned the Lord
about my dilemma.
"Lord, you told me when I decided to follow You,
You would walk and talk with me all the way.
But I'm aware that during the most troublesome
times of my life there is only one set of footprints.
I just don't understand why, when I needed You most,
You leave me."
He whispered, "My precious child,
I love you and will never leave you
never, ever, during your trials and testings.
When you saw only one set of footprints
it was then that I carried you."

Margaret Fishback Powers

Copyright ©1964 by Margaret Fishback Powers.

Through a Child's Eyes

An old man sat in his rocker day after day.

Fixated in his chair, he promised not to remove himself from this spot until he saw God.

On one fine spring afternoon, the old man rocking in his chair, relentless in his visual quest of God, saw a young girl playing across the street. The little girl's ball rolled into the old man's yard. She ran to pick it up and as she bent down to reach for the ball, she looked at the old man and said, "Mr. Old Man, I see you every day rocking in your chair and staring off into nothing. What is it that you are looking for?"

"Oh, my dear child, you are yet too young to understand," replied the old man.

"Maybe," replied the young girl, "but my momma always told me if I had something in my head I should talk about it. She says to get a better understanding. My momma always says 'Miss Lizzy share your thoughts.' Share, share, share, my momma always says."

"Oh, well, Miss Lizzy child, I do not think you could help me," grunted the old man.

"Possibly not, Mr. Old Man, sir, but maybe I can help just listening."

"All right, Miss Lizzy child, I am looking for God."

"With all due respect, Mr. Old Man, sir, you rock

back and forth in that chair day after day in search of God?" Miss Lizzy responded, puzzled.

"Why, yes. I need to believe before my death that there is a God. I need a sign and I have yet to have seen one," said the old man.

"A sign, sir? A sign?" said Miss Lizzy, now quite confused by the old man's words. "Mr. Old Man, sir, God gives you a sign when you breathe your next breath. When you can smell fresh flowers. When you can hear the birds sing. When all of the babies are born. Sir, God gives you a sign when you laugh and when you cry, when you feel the tears roll from your eyes. It is a sign in your heart to hug and to love. God gives you a sign in the wind and in the rainbows and the change in the seasons. All of the signs are there, but do you not believe in them? Mr. Old Man, sir, God is in you and God is in me. There is no searching because he, she or whatever may be is just here all of the time."

With one hand on her hip and the other hand flailing about the air, Miss Lizzy continued, "Momma says, 'Miss Lizzy, if you are searching for something monumental, you have closed your eyes because to see God is to see simple things, to see God is to see life in all things.' That is what Momma says."

"Miss Lizzy, child, you are quite insightful in your knowledge of God, but this that you speak of is yet not quite enough."

Lizzy walked up to the old man and placed her young childish hands over his heart and spoke softly into his ear. "Sir, it comes from in here, not out there," pointing to the sky. "Find it in your heart, in your own mirror. Then, Mr. Old Man, sir, you will see the signs."

Miss Lizzy, walking back across the street, turned to the old man and smiled. Then, as she bent down to smell the flowers, she shouted, "Momma always says, 'Miss Lizzy, if you are looking for something monumental, you have closed your eyes.'"

Dee Dee Robinson

A Sense of a Goose

Next fall, when you see geese heading south for the winter, flying along in "V" formation, you might consider what science has discovered as to why they fly that way. As each bird flaps its wings, it creates an uplift for the bird immediately following. By flying in "V" formation, the whole flock adds at least 71 percent greater flying range than if each bird flew on its own.

People who share a common direction and sense of community can get where they are going more quickly and easily, because they are traveling on the thrust of one another.

When a goose falls out of formation, it suddenly feels the drag and resistance of trying to go it alone—and quickly gets back into formation to take advantage of the lifting power of the bird in front.

If we have as much sense as a goose, we will stay in formation with those people who are headed the same way we are.

When the head goose gets tired, it rotates back in the wing and another goose flies point.

It is sensible to take turns doing demanding jobs, whether with people or with geese flying south.

Geese honk from behind to encourage those up front to keep up their speed.

What messages do we give when we honk from behind?

Finally—and this is important—when a goose gets sick or is wounded by gunshot, and falls out of formation, two other geese fall out with that goose and follow it down to lend help and protection. They stay with the fallen goose until it is able to fly or until it dies; and only then do they launch out on their own, or with another formation to catch up with their group.

If we have the sense of a goose, we will stand by each other like that.

Author Unknown

I Know He Goes to War

I can't tell you of ever finding God in church
and I can't remember feeling He was near me
    when I went there.

I do remember seeing a lot of friendly smiling faces
and people dressed in all their nice clothes.
Somehow, I always felt uneasy—too many people,
    too close.

No, I don't remember seeing God in church
but I hear His name there constantly.
Some ask, "Have you been born again?
If so, when?" And I don't understand!

I did feel God in Vietnam—
almost every day.

I felt Him when, after an all-night fire fight,
He sent the sun to chase the rain away; and the rain
would return with majesty the very next day.

He was there when I collected Sergeant Moore's body
    parts to put in a body bag.
He was there when I wrote a letter to his widow
    explaining how he died.
He was behind me when I heard Sergeant Sink's last
    dying gasp.

He helped me carry Sergeant Swanson down a hill in
   the An Loe Valley.

I caught a glimpse of God when I felt the heat of napalm
called on our own position, May 27, 1967.

I felt Him around me when
the chaplain would hold field services for our dead.

I saw His reflection in the faces of my men
when I told them to save one bullet for themselves
as we were about to be overrun one hot steamy day
   in a 'Nam far away.

He led me in the Lord's Prayer on every air assault
as we stood on the skids coming in at treetop level.

When we set up our night ambushes
and I couldn't see my own hands because of the darkness,
I would feel His hands.

He sent loneliness to guarantee the fond memories
that always appear later in life.

I'll always remember the strength God gave to the orphans—
the children of war.
He made them strong, but they didn't understand.
I know after 25 years, we sleep under the same star.

He sent boys to war. They returned young men;
their lives forever changed,
proud to protect the land
of the free.

I don't know if God goes to church,
but I know He goes to war.

Dr. Barry L. McAlpine
First Squadron
Ninth U.S. Cavalry

The Bike Ride

Life is like riding a bicycle. You don't fall off unless you stop pedaling.
Claude Pepper   U.S.
                                                    Congressman

At first I saw God as an observer, like my judge, keeping track of things I did wrong. This way, God would know whether I merited heaven or hell when I died. He was always out there, sort of like the President. I recognized His picture when I saw it, but I didn't really know Him at all.

But later on, when I recognized my higher power better, it seemed as though life was rather like a bike ride, on a tandem bike, and I noticed God was in the back helping me pedal.

I don't know when it was that He suggested we change places, but life has not been the same since.... life with my higher power, that is, making life much more exciting.

When I had control, I knew the way. It was rather boring but predictable. It was always the shortest distance between the points.

But when He took the lead, He knew delightful cuts, up mountains, and through rocky places and at breakneck speeds; it was all I could do to hang on!

Even though it looked like madness, He kept saying, "Pedal, pedal!"

I worried and became anxious, asking, "Where are you taking me?" He just laughed and didn't answer, and I found myself starting to trust. I soon forgot my boring life and entered into the adventure, and when I'd say, "I'm scared," He'd lean back and touch my hand.

He took me to people with gifts that I needed; gifts of healing, acceptance and joy. They gave me their gifts to take on my journey. *Our* journey, that is, God's and mine.

And we were off again. He said, "Give the gifts away, they're extra baggage, too much weight." So I did, to the people we met, and I found that in giving *I* received, and still our burden was light.

I did not trust Him at first, in control of my life. I thought He'd wreck it. But He knew *bike secrets*, knew how to make it bend to take sharp corners, jump to clear places filled with rocks, fly to shorten scary passages.

And I'm learning to shut up and pedal in the strangest places, and I'm beginning to enjoy the view and the cool breeze on my face with my delightful constant companion, *my higher power*.

And when I'm sure I can't go on anymore, He just smiles and says, "Pedal . . ."

Author Unknown

Who Is Jack Canfield?

Jack Canfield is one of America's leading experts in the development of human potential and personal effectiveness. He is both a dynamic, entertaining speaker and a highly sought-after trainer. Jack has a wonderful ability to inform and inspire audiences toward increased levels of self-esteem and peak performance.

He is the author and narrator of several bestselling audio- and videocassette programs, including *Self-Esteem and Peak Performance, How to Build High Self-Esteem, Self-Esteem in the Classroom* and *Chicken Soup for the Soul—Live.* He is regularly seen on television shows such as *Good Morning America, 20/20* and *NBC Nightly News.* Jack has coauthored numerous books, including the *Chicken Soup for the Soul* series, *Dare to Win* and *The Aladdin Factor* (all with Mark Victor Hansen), *100 Ways to Build Self-Concept in the Classroom* (with Harold C. Wells) and *Heart at Work* (with Jacqueline Miller).

Jack is a regularly featured speaker for professional associations, school districts, government agencies, churches, hospitals, sales organizations and corporations. His clients have included the American Dental Association, the American Management Association, AT&T, Campbell Soup, Clairol, Domino's Pizza, GE, ITT, Hartford Insurance, Johnson & Johnson, the Million Dollar Roundtable, NCR, New England Telephone, Re/Max, Scott Paper, TRW and Virgin Records. Jack is also on the faculty of Income Builders International, a school for entrepreneurs.

Jack conducts an annual eight-day Training of Trainers program in the areas of self-esteem and peak performance. It attracts educators, counselors, parenting trainers, corporate trainers, professional speakers, ministers and others interested in developing their speaking and seminar-leading skills.

For further information about Jack's books, tapes and training programs, or to schedule him for a presentation, please contact:

The Canfield Training Group
P.O. Box 30880 • Santa Barbara, CA 93130
phone: 805-563-2935 • fax: 805-563-2945
To e-mail or visit our Web site:
http://www.chickensoup.com

Who Is Mark Victor Hansen?

Mark Victor Hansen is a professional speaker who, in the last twenty years, has made over four-thousand presentations to more than 2 million people in thirty-two countries. His presentations cover sales excellence and strategies; personal empowerment and development; and how to triple your income and double your time off.

Mark has spent a lifetime dedicated to his mission of making a profound and positive difference in people's lives. Throughout his career, he has inspired hundreds of thousands of people to create a more powerful and purposeful future for themselves while stimulating the sale of billions of dollars worth of goods and services.

Mark is a prolific writer and has authored *Future Diary, How to Achieve Total Prosperity* and *The Miracle of Tithing.* He is coauthor of the *Chicken Soup for the Soul* series, *Dare to Win* and *The Aladdin Factor* (all with Jack Canfield) and *The Master Motivator* (with Joe Batten).

Mark has also produced a complete library of personal empowerment audio- and videocassette programs that have enabled his listeners to recognize and use their innate abilities in their business and personal lives. His message has made him a popular television and radio personality, with appearances on ABC, NBC, CBS, HBO, PBS and CNN. He has also appeared on the cover of numerous magazines, including *Success, Entrepreneur* and *Changes.*

Mark is a big man with a heart and spirit to match—an inspiration to all who seek to better themselves.

For further information about Mark write:

P.O. Box 7665
Newport Beach, CA 92658
phone: 714-759-9304 or 800-433-2314
fax: 714-722-6912
Web site: http://www.chickensoup.com

Contributors

Many of the stories in this book were taken from books we have read. Some of the stories and poems were contributed by friends of ours, who, like us, are professional speakers. If you would like to contact them for information on their books, tapes and seminars, you can reach them at the addresses and phone numbers provided below.

Many of the stories were also contributed by readers like yourself, who, after reading the first volume of *Chicken Soup for the Soul*, were inspired to submit a story out of their life's experience. We have included information about them as well.

Raymond L. Aaron is a captivating speaker in the fields of real estate, business and motivation. A household name across Canada and an entry in the prestigious Canadian Who's Who, Mr. Aaron has helped tens of thousands of fellow Canadians dramatically increase their wealth through creative purchases of real estate. To attend his courses or purchase his various motivational audiotapes, write The Raymond Aaron Group at 9225 Leslie Street, #2, Richmond Hill, Ontario, Canada L4B 3H6 or fax at (905) 881-8996.

Steve Andreas has been a searcher and wanderer most of his life. As part of this continuing journey, he has been a learner, teacher, therapist, author, publisher, husband and parent.

Ralph Archbold has been speaking since 1983 in an award-winning portrayal of Benjamin Franklin for corporate and convention groups. For information about the topics he addresses, contact him at Ben Franklin, PO Box 40178, Philadelphia, PA 19106. Call 215-238-0871 or fax 215-238-9102.

Ken Blanchard, Ph.D., is chairman of Blanchard Training and Development, a full-service management consulting and training company. He is the author of numerous books, including the all-time bestseller *The One Minute Manager*. A sought-after speaker and business consultant, he can be reached at Blanchard Training and Development, 125 State Place, Escondido, CA 92029. Call 1-800-728-6000.

Harold H. Bloomfield, M.D., is one of the leading psychological educators of our time. He has written numerous books, including *How to Survive The Loss of a Love, Making Peace with Your Parents, Making Peace with Yourself, How to Heal Depression* and *The Power of Five*. He is also a sought-after keynote speaker. For further information, please contact him at 1110 Luneta Drive, Del Mar, CA 92014. Call 619-481-9950 or fax 619-792-2333.

Lisa Boyd resides in Del Mar, California, with her husband and two children. She is very active in various volunteer activities and enjoys craftwork and writing poetry. Lisa can be reached by writing P.O. Box 2070, Del Mar, California 92014 or by calling (619) 755-2120. Fax (619) 755-9242.

Mike Buettell a highly respected junior high school counselor in Irvine,

California. Partially disabled, he is a living inspiration to his students that courage, perseverance, and a sense of humor can overcome any obstacle. He can be reached at Rancho Middle School, 4861 Michelson, Irvine, CA 92715. Call 714-786-3005.

Ben Burton is a humorist, speaker and writer residing in Hot Springs, Arkansas. *The Matyrdom of Andy* is excerpted from Ben Burton's new book, *The Chicken That Won a Dogfight*. He can be reached at 10 Queens Row, Hot Springs, AR 71901. Call 501-623-6496.

Bruce Carmichael spent his early years on a family farm in northern Missouri. He received his degree at Northwest Missouri State University, was a decorated fighter pilot in WW II, a high school principal, and later earned degrees in both medicine and chiropractic. He is now practicing chiropractic in the Missouri Ozarks.

John Catenacci is just another being of the human type, dancing through life with his Army boots on. A practicing chemical engineer, he is also a community and environmental activist, published writer and an organizational development/team-building consultant. He can be reached at 1355 S. Winter St. Apt A-4, Adrian, MI 49221. Call 517-265-6138 (day).

Dan Clark is the International Ambassador of the "Art of Being Alive." He has spoken to over 2 million people in all fifty states, Canada, Europe, Asia and Russia. Dan is an actor, songwriter, recording artist, video producer and award-winning athlete. He is the well-known author of six books, including *Getting High—How to Really Do It, One Minute Messages* and *The Art of Being Alive*. He can be reached at P.O. Box 8689, Salt Lake City, UT 84108 or call 801-485-5755.

Charles A. Coonradt is the author of *The Game of Work* and *Managing the Obvious*. Both books are referred to as management "must reads." His company, The Game of Work, Inc., has been improving productivity and profitability for its clients since 1973. He is recognized as an author, speaker and consultant. He can be reached at 1912 Sidewinder Drive, Suite 201, Park City, UT 84060. Call 800-438-6074.

Stan Dale, formerly the voice of "The Shadow" and the announcer/narrator of "The Lone Ranger," "Sgt. Preston" and "The Green Hornet" radio shows, is the Director/Founder of the Human Awareness Institute in San Mateo, CA. He conducts "Sex, Love and Intimacy Workshops" around the world. Stan is the author of *Fantasies Can Set You Free* and *My Child, My Self: How to Raise the Child You Always Wanted to Be*. Both books are available from The Human Awareness Institute, 1720 S. Amphlett Blvd., Suite 128, San Mateo, CA 94402. Call 800-800-4117 or 415-571-5524.

Beverly K. Fine was first prize winner of Maryland Poetry Society. She has had essays published in *The Sun Magazine*, *The Anchorage Daily News*, and *The Baltimore Evening Sun*. She also had poems published in *Our World's Best Loved Poems*, ed. John Campbell. Beverly is a member of Delta Epsilon Sigma, National Scholastic Honor Society, Alpha Delta Chapter, and Honor Society.

Pam Finger is a workshop facilitator and consultant who specializes in self-esteem and values clarification issues. She is the president of the Rochester chapter of the National Council for Self-Esteem and is president and co-founder of Inner-Trek, a training and consulting organization based in Rochester, New York. She may be contacted through Inner Trek, PO Box 32, Fairport, NY 14450. Call 716-223-0153 or fax 716-223-0147.

Bob Fox, The Old Bluebird, is a newspaper columnist for the Brookville Star in Brookville, Ohio. He led the Brookville High School Bluebirds to a state championship in 1935 and went on to play amateur, semi-pro and minor league baseball. He can be reached by writing PO Box 43, Brookville, OH 45309, or call (513) 833-4396.

Stan Gebhardt is president of CompuQuest Educational Services, a global leader in computer education programs for children and adults. A public speaker, poet and singer, he addresses a variety of audiences and can be reached at 614-888-4900.

H. Stephen Glenn is an internationally acclaimed family psychologist who speaks to over 100,000 people each year. Steve has written numerous books and courses including *Raising Self-Reliant Children in a Self-Indulgent World* and *Positive Discipline in the Classroom* as well as several outstanding training series, including Developing Capable People, and Basic Substance Abuse Counseling. He is president of Capabilities, Inc. and can be reached at PO Box 2515, Fair Oaks, CA 95628, or call 916-961-5556.

Ted Goff is a cartoonist in Kansas City. He may be reached at P.O.Box 22679, Kansas City, MO 64113.

D.H. Groberg has lived, worked and presented all over the world; first as director of training for Mobil Oil's international operations, as founding vice-president for international and key facilitator for Stephen Covey's *Seven Habits of Highly Effective People;* and as independent speaker/presen-ter/facilitator on such topics as *Five Moments of Truth, Values Across Cultures, Inner Productivity* and other inspirational/motivational topics. Contact him at 2163 Lorita Way, Sandy, UT 84093. Call 801-943-5529, fax 801-943-3700.

Patty Hansen has her priorities straight—being Mom is number one. As the other half of the "Mark/Patty Team," she devotes her time between being Chief Financial Officer and trouble-shooter at M.V. Hansen & Associates, Inc., and full-time driver, caretaker and homework assistant to their two daughters, Elisabeth and Melanie. She also loves to squeeze in some time to garden, raise chickens and play on the beach. She is currently at work on her first book. She can be reached at PO Box 7665, Newport Beach, CA 92658. Call 714-759-9304.

Bob Harris is a professional development trainer and keynote speaker in business and education. Bob's audio programs include *What's The Magnitude of Your Attitude?, How to Create Dreams Worth Living* and *Self-Esteem the Same in Any Language.* Bob can be reached at Bob Harris & Assoc., 5942 Edinger Avenue, Ste. 113, Huntington Beach, CA 92649. Call 1-800-TO-EXCEED.

Rob and Toni Harris are the owners of Re/Max Results Realtors and the proud parents of Nick. Nick has been raised to be a positive thinker, with a strong belief in himself. They reside at 11630 Woodstone Place, Fort Wayne, IN 46845. Call 219-482-7090.

D. Trinidad Hunt is an educator, international speaker and sought-after corporate trainer and consultant. Her solid business success tools shared in her Learning to Learn: Maximizing Your Performance Potential book and audio series have propelled numerous companies from mediocrity into organizational excellence. Trin can be reached at Elan Enterprises, 47-430 Hui Nene St., Kaneohe, HI 96744. Call 800-707-3526 or fax 808-239-2482.

Larry James is a professional speaker and author of the book *How to Really Love the One You're With.* He travels across the nation, leading seminars and presenting keynotes of inspiration that focus on personal and professional relationship development and business networking. Contact Larry James at Career Assurance Network, P.O. Box 35294, Tulsa, OK 74153-0294. Call 918-744-9223 or 800-725-9223.

Avril Johannes was born in England and is a professional aviculturalist. Author of short stories published in *Alaska Magazine* and various newspapers, she is presently working on a book of short stories about Alaska, where she lived for 20 years. She can be reached at 8070 New Hope Rd., Grants Pass, OR 97527.

Leadership ... with a human touch is a pocket-size magazine published every four weeks by The Economics Press, 12 Daniel Road, Fairfield, NJ 07004. It contains short anecdotes and common sense advice about the art of leading and dealing with people in the workplace and in the community. In addition, subscribers can expect a lot of humor and an occasional poignant story to lift their spirits. For a free sample issue, write Arthur F. Lenehan, Editor, at the above address, or call toll free 1-800-526-2554 or FAX (201) 227-9742 for subscription information.

Art Linkletter has been a television and radio star for more than 60 years. He has won two Emmy Awards and received four Emmy nominations, a Grammy Award and ten honorary doctorate degrees. He has written 23 books. Art has served on President Nixon's National Advisory Council for Drug Abuse Prevention and on the Presidential Commission to improve reading in the United States. He can be reached at 8484 Wilshire Blvd., Ste. 205, Beverly Hills, CA 90211. Call 213-658-7603 or fax 213-655-5173.

Donna Loesch is an inspiring speaker as well as a writer/producer of motivational products for empowerment through self-love and positive self-talk (videos, books and cassettes). She is president and founder of Creative Dreams for Self-Esteem, Monterey, California. Write to her at 1152 East 3200 South, Bountiful, UT 84010 or call 801-295-7313.

Diane Loomans is a dynamic speaker and best selling author who speaks internationally on the topics of self-esteem, communication and the power of laughter and play. She has written *Full Esteem Ahead: 100 Ways to Build Self-Esteem in Children & Adults, The Laughing Classroom: Everyone's Guide to Teaching with Humor & Play, The Lovables in the Kingdom of Self-Esteem, Positively Mother Goose,* and *Today I am Lovable.* She is a frequent guest on national radio and television, and is the President of Global Learning, PO Box 1203, Solana Beach, CA 92075. Call (619) 944-9842.

Patricia Lorenz is an inspirational writer, columnist, writing teacher and speaker. Of her articles and stories, 400 have appeared in over 70 publications including *Reader's Digest, Guideposts, Working Mother* and *Single-Parent Family*. "But mostly," Pat says, "I'm a mom from Oak Creek, Wisconsin who loves to write." You can write to her at 7457 S. Pennsylvania Avenue, Oak Creek, WI 53154.

Tony Luna is founder of Tony Luna Creative Services. He is also an instructor at the Art Center College of Design in the field of creativity and business. Tony is a member of the board of directors of U.P., a non-profit organization dedicated to empowering young people through the arts by promoting talented youth into education and employment in the creative industries. You may reach him at 819 North Bel Aire Drive, Burbank, CA 91501-1205. Call 818-842-5490.

John Magliola Jr. graduated S.C.C.C. Cum Laude and was elected to the ranks of *Who's Who in American Junior Colleges*. He also holds a Bachelor of Arts degree from the University of New Haven. He can be reached by calling 203-269-5352.

Lisa Manley is in the business of promoting individuals who are working to make the world a better place. She presents their ideas and causes through a variety of media, including audio-cassettes, videos, graphics and writing. You can contact her at Coral Communications, PO Box 5243, Balboa Island, CA 92662. Call 714-675-9989.

Dennis E. Mannering for 45 years has researched the mysteries of life, searching for ways to live more fully and to help others get more out of their lives. In the past 15 years, Dennis has spoken to over 150,000 individuals, sharing these experiences with them. He is the author of *How Good Managers Become Great Leaders*, plus several audio-cassette albums, including *Motivation in Action*. He may be reached at Options Unlimited, Inc., 617 Sunrise Lane, Green Bay, WI 54305. Call 800-236-3445.

Dr. Barry McAlpine graduated from Palmer College of Chiropractic in 1971. He enjoys a very successful chiropractic practice in Holland, Michigan. He can be reached by calling 616-392-7031.

Hanoch McCarty, Ed.D., is an educational psychologist, author and nationally known public speaker. His keynote addresses, seminars and workshops are noted for their high energy, great humor, participant involvement and perceptive insights. He is co-author, with Meladee McCarty, of the bestselling books, *Acts of Kindness: How to Create a Kindness Revolution* and *A Year of Kindness: 365 Ways to Spread Sunshine*. He can be reached at 209-745-2212.

Meladee McCarty is a program specialist at the Sacramento County Office of Education. She finds placements for severely handicapped children and works with families, teachers and children in a special-education setting. She is co-author, with Hanoch McCarty, of *Acts of Kindness: How to Create a Kindness Revolution* and *A Year of Kindness: 365 Ways to Spread Sunshine*.. She can be reached at 1-800-KINDNESS.

Glenn McIntyre, founder of Creating Magic, is unique: a police officer, a nationally ranked wheelchair tennis player, and an inspiring speaker/consultant who, along with his talented service dog, Merlin, helps businesses and public agencies address the needs and opportunities of the disabled community. A nationally known expert on the Americans with Disabilities Act, Glenn teaches how to capture the "almost untouched market" of persons with disabilities, while complying with regulatory requirements in a common-sense, low stress, cost-effective manner. Glenn can be reached at 6349 Via Cozumel, Camarillo, CA 93012, or call 805-388-2352.

Jann Mitchell is a feature writer for *The Oregonian* in Portland, Oregon. She has received national awards for her coverage of social issues, features, humor and mental health. Her popular Sunday column, "Relating," provides insights into our relationships with others and ourselves. She is the author of two books, *Codependent for Sure* and *Organized Serenity*. She also lectures frequently on self-development.

Nancy Moorman has been conducting dynamic staff development, parenting and student presentations across the nation for 10 years. She has co-authored the book, *Teacher Talk: What It Really Means* and has available numerous books, articles and videotapes. You can contact Nancy at PO Box 1130, Bay City, MI 48706. Call 517-686-3251.

Stanley D. Moulson is a recovering alcoholic from Aurora, Ontario, Canada, who has chosen a path of self-improvement and self-awareness. On this journey he has worked with Raymond Aaron, real estate guru, Robert Allen and Wright Thurston. Stanley's story, "Love Never Leaves You," was written after reading *Chicken Soup for the Soul* which gave him the courage to open up and share this story for the first time.

Erik Olesen is a professional speaker, psychotherapist and author who helps people become more confident, relaxed and productive. He has spoken for over 80 organizations throughout North America. Olesen's book, *Mastering the Winds of Change: Peak Performers Reveal How to Stay on Top in Times of Turmoil* (Harper Collins) features a complete conditioning program for mastering the pressure of change in the 1990s and beyond. His book for children, *The Little Sailboat and the Big Storm* (Coming of Age Press) helps kids become more confident and optimistic. To order books, or to contact Erik Olesen, please write to 2740 Fulton, Suite 203, Sacramento, CA 95821, or call, toll-free, 1-800-STRONG-U.

Carol Lynn Pearson is widely known for her books of poetry, most recently *Women I Have Known and Been. Goodbye, I Love You* tells of her life with a homosexual husband who ultimately died of AIDS. She wrote the popular Christmas book, *The Modern Magi*, and has performed internationally her one-women play, "Mother Wove the Morning," a search for the female face of God. She can be reached at (510) 939-0757; 1384 Cornwall Ct., Walnut Creek, CA 94596.

Willa Perrier, a native of Louisiana, writes historical events in verse. Her love of poetry is recorded in early life through recitations and writings. She is a retired educator with experience ranging from primary grades to the junior-college level in both her native state and in California.

Dawn Philips lives near Rocky Mountain House, Alberta. She attended the University of Alberta, taught in one-room schools, and developed programs to integrate special needs children into regular school systems. She is married with four children, eight grandchildren and one great-grandchild.

Pastor John R. Ramsey is a highly acclaimed pastor with a motivational message that has propelled him into one of America's fastest growing ministries. His weekly television show can be seen in four states and in over 800,000 homes. He can be reached at John Ramsey Ministries, 3238 E Hwy 390, Panama City, FL 32405-9305. Call 904-271-9647.

Robert Reasoner is a highly respected educator and international authority on self-esteem and motivation. He currently holds the office of president of the International Council for Self-Esteem. He is the author of *Building Self-Esteem: A Comprehensive Program for Schools*. He can be contacted at 234 Montgomery Lane, Ft. Ludlow, WA 98365. Call 206-437-0300.

Dee Dee Robinson has worked at a small restaurant for the last five years in Atlanta, Georgia. She is renowned speaker and author on the subject of spirituality and self-love. Dee Dee started writing about five years ago and enjoys sharing her writing with others. She can be reached by writing to 2644 Marietta, GA 30067 or by calling 404-973-0422.

Jim Rohn has focused on the fundamentals of human behavior that most affect personal and business performance for more than 30 years. He now concentrates his creative skills on Jim Rohn International, a diversified corporation engaged in the worldwide marketing of personal development, management and sales-oriented seminars and training programs. In addition to his best-selling books, *Seasons of Life* and *The Seven Strategies for Wealth and Happiness*, he has recently written *The Five Major Pieces to the Life Puzzle*. He can be reached at 9810 North MacArthur Boulevard, Suite 303, Irving, TX 75063, or by calling 214-401-1000.

Bill Sanders has shared the speaking platform with Presidents Ford and Reagan, Zig Ziglar and others. He has written 14 books and is the host of TV's only teen talk show, "Straight Talk," shown in 43 million homes. To contact Bill for your school or business talk or seminar, write to him at Bill Sanders Speeches, 8495 Valleywood Lane, Kalamazoo, MI 49002. Call 616-323-8074.

John Wayne Schlatter is a speaker whose topics are inspirational, full of insight and rich with his own special brand of humor. Jack is a former speech and drama teacher as well as an author of many works. Jack was listed in the 1990 edition of *Who's Who Among Teachers in America*. He is a member of the Professionals Speakers Network. In 1993, he was honored by his peers with the prestigious Speaker of the Year Award. Jack can be reached at P.O. Box 577, Cypress, CA 90630. Call 714-879-7271.

Floyd Shilanski is a recognized and dynamic speaker, motivational trainer, and sales person who travels internationally doing money management seminars and workshops for schools, organizations, and other sales organizations. Floyd is well known for his simple approach to managing your money. He is the author of *Learn to Win at the Money Game* and can be reached by writing to Shilanski and Associates, Inc., 236 W. 10th Avenue, Anchorage, AK 99501 or by calling 907-278-1351.

Marlon Smith the "high-tech" motivator, is a fitting name for who is utilizing his electrical engineering background to empower individuals. Using innovative multi-media presentations, he entertains, inspires and motivates everyone through his unique program to incorporate a systemic process for reinforcing the keynote message long after his presentation. Marlon has developed the *Help Me! Series: A Solution Guide for Today's Youth.* This motivational program includes 13 workbooks, audio tapes, instructional video and teacher-parent lesson plans. Marlon holds a Bachelor of Science degree from the University of Virginia in electrical engineering. His corporate experience includes working for two Fortune-500 corporations, IBM and Hewlett-Packard. He can be reached by writing Success By Choice, 25125 Santa Clara Street, Suite #321, Hayward, CA 94544 or call (510) 887-1311.

Dottie Walters is the president of the Walters International Speakers Bureau in California. She is the author of *The Greatest Speakers I Have Ever Heard*, featuring Jack Canfield and Mark Victor Hansen; and *Speak and Grow Rich* with her daughter, Lilly. She is founder of The International Group of Agents and Bureaus and she is the editor/publisher of *Sharing Ideas* news magazine—the largest in the world for paid professional speakers. She can be reached at PO Box 1120, Glendora, CA 91740. Call 818-335-8069 or fax 818-335-6127.

Lilly Walters is the executive director of Walters International Speakers Bureau, a professional lecture agency with 20,000 world-famous celebrities and interesting and entertaining business speakers. She has authored many books, videos and audio albums, including *Secrets of Successful Speakers—How You Can Motivate, Captivate and Persuade; What to Say When You're Dyin' on the Platform!; Speak and Grow Rich* and many others. Call 818-335-8069 or fax 818-335-6127.

Larry Winget is a motivational humorist, business speaker and author of several books, including *Money Stuff*, which ties the spiritual principles of love, service and giving straight to the bottom line, and *Stuff That Works Every Single Day*. His personal story of triumph over financial disaster and his hilarious business stories make him a sought-after convention speaker. He can be contacted at Win Seminars! PO Box 700485, Tulsa, OK 74170. Call 800-749-4597.

Bettie B. Youngs, Ph.D., Ed.D., is one of the nation's most respected voices on the role of self-esteem as it detracts or empowers vitality in health, achievement and personal growth for both children and adults. She is also highly regarded for her knowledge of developmental stages and their contribution to meaning, purpose and actualizing potential. Bettie is the author of 14 books published in 27 languages including *How to Develop Self-Esteem in Your Child, Safeguarding Your Teenager from the Dragons of Life,* and *Values from the Heartland: Stories of an American Farmgirl*. She can be contacted at Bettie B. Youngs & Associates, 3060 Racetrack View Drive, Del Mar, CA 92014. Call 619-481-6360.

Permissions

The Two-Dollar Bill. Reprinted by permission of Floyd Shilanski. ©1994 Floyd Shilanski.

Do It Now! Reprinted by permission of Dennis Mannering. From the book *Attitudes Are Contagious . . . Are Yours Worth Catching?* ©1986 by Dennis E. Mannering.

The Heart, The Annual Letters, and *Let's Walk Through the Garden Again.* Reprinted by permission of Raymond Aaron. ©1994 Raymond Aaron.

The Baggy Yellow Shirt. Reprinted by permission of Patricia Lorenz. ©1993 Patricia Lorenz.

The Flower. Reprinted by permission of Pastor John R. Ramsey. ©1994 Pastor John R. Ramsey.

Practice Random Kindness and Senseless Acts of Beauty. Used by permission of Adair Lara. ©1991 Adair Lara. This article originally appeared in *Glamour.*

A Life Worth Saving, Two Brothers and *The Optimist.* Reprinted from *More Sower's Seeds* by Brian Cavanaugh, T.O.R. ©1990 by Brian Cavanaugh, T.O.R. Used by permission of Paulist Press.

Heaven and Hell—The Real Difference and *My Father When I Was . . .* Permission granted by Ann Landers/Creators Syndicate.

Grandmother's Gift. Reprinted by permission of D. Trinidad Hunt. ©1994 D. Trinidad Hunt.

Angels Don't Need Legs to Fly. Reprinted by permission of Stan Dale. ©1994 Stan Dale.

The Little Glass Chip and *Graduation, Inheritance & Other Lessons.* Reprinted by permission of Bettie B. Youngs. Excerpted from *Values from the Heartland: Stories of an American Farmgirl.* ©1994 Bettie B. Youngs.

The Martyrdom of Andy. Reprinted by permission of Ben Burton. ©1994 Ben Burton.

If I Had My Child to Raise Over Again. From the book *Full Esteem Ahead* by Diane Loomans with Julia Loomans. Reprinted by permission of H J Kramer c/o Global Learning, Box 1203, Solana Beach, CA 92075. All rights reserved.

He Is Just a Little Boy. Reprinted by permission of Bob Fox. ©1994 Bob Fox.

Will You, Daddy? Reprinted by permission of Michael Foster. ©1994 Michael Foster.

But You Didn't. Reprinted by permission of Stan Gebhardt. ©1994 Stan Gebhardt.

The Spirit of Santa Doesn't Wear a Red Suit and *Suki . . . A Best Friend for All*

Reasons. Reprinted by permission of Patty Hansen. ©1994 Patty Hansen.

The Little Lady Who Changed My Life. Reprinted by permission of Tony Luna. ©1994 Tony Luna.

10th Row Center. Reprinted by permission of Jim Rohn. ©1994 Jim Rohn.

The Gift. Reprinted by permission of John Catenacci. ©1994 John Catenacci.

She Remembered. Reprinted by permission of Lisa Boyd. ©1994 Lisa Boyd.

Rescued. Used by permission of *Leadership . . . with a human touch.* Published by The Economics Press, Inc.

Go Into the Light. Reprinted by permission of Donna Loesch. ©1994 Donna Loesch.

A Chaplain's Gift. Reprinted by permission of Dawn Philips. ©1995 Dawn Philips. Originally appeared in *Legion* magazine, Ottawa, Ontario, Canada.

Do It Today! Reprinted by permission of Robert Reasoner. ©1994 Robert Reasoner.

Remembering Ms. Murphy. Reprinted by permission of Beverly Fine. ©1994 Beverly Fine.

An Act of Kindness for a Broken Heart. Reprinted by permission of Meladee McCarty. ©1994 Meladee McCarty.

See You in the Morning, The Magic Pebbles and *The Finest Steel Gets Sent Through the Hottest Furnace.* Reprinted by permission of John Wayne Schlatter. ©1994 John Wayne Schlatter.

Love Never Leaves You. Reprinted by permission of Stanley D. Moulson. ©1994 Stanley D. Moulson.

The Prettiest Angel. Reprinted by permission of Ralph Archbold. ©1994 Ralph Archbold.

A Place to Stand. Reprinted by permission of Charles Garfield. ©1994 Charles Garfield.

Attitude—One of Life's Choices. Reprinted by permission of Bob Harris. ©1994 Bob Harris.

We're the Retards. Condensed from "Don't Waste Your Time With Those Kids," by Janice Anderson Connolly, from the book, *The First Year of Teaching.* Edited by Pearl Rock Cane. ©1991 by Pearl Rock Cane. Reprinted with permission from Walker and Company, 435 Hudson St., New York, NY 10014, 1-800-289-2553. All rights reserved.

What's Happening with Today's Youth? Reprinted by permission of Marlon Smith. ©1994 Marlon Smith.

A Simple Touch. Reprinted by permission of Nancy Moorman. ©1994 Nancy Moorman

As a Man Soweth. Reprinted by permission of Mike Buetelle. ©1994 Mike Buetelle.

A Small Boy. Reprinted by permission of John Magliola. ©1994 John Magliola.

A Little Girl's Dream. Reprinted by permission of Jann Mitchell. ©1994 Jann Mitchell.

A Salesman's First Sale. Reprinted by permission of Rob, Toni and Nick Harris. ©1994 Rob, Toni and Nick Harris.

The Cowboy's Story. Reprinted by permission of Larry Winget. ©1994 Larry Winget.

Why Wait? . . . Just Do It! Reprinted by permission of Glenn McIntyre. ©1994 Glenn McIntyre.

Thirty-Nine Years–Too Short–Too Long–Long Enough. Reprinted by permission of Willa Perrier. ©1994 Willa Perrier.

Nothing But Problems. Reprinted by permission of Ken Blanchard. ©1994 Ken Blanchard.

Angels Never Say "Hello." Reprinted by permission of Dottie Walters. ©1994 Dottie Walters.

Why Do These Things Have to Happen? Reprinted by permission of Lilly Walters. ©1994 Lilly Walters.

The Race. Reprinted by permission of D.H. Groberg. © 1994 D.H. Groberg.

Summit America. Reprinted by permission of Lisa Manley. ©1994 Lisa Manley.

An Undiscovered Masterpiece. Reprinted by permission of Charles A. Coonradt. ©1994 Charles Coonradt.

If I Could Do It, You Can Too! Reprinted by permission of Art Linkletter. ©1994 Art Linkletter.

Napoleon and the Furrier. Reprinted by permission of Steve Andreas. ©1990 Steve Andreas.

Footprints. Reprinted by permission of HarperCollins Publishers, Ltd. Copyright ©1964 by Margaret Fishback Powers.

Through a Child's Eyes. Reprinted by permission of Dee Dee Robinson. ©1994 Dee Dee Robinson.

I Know He Goes to War. Reprinted by permission of Dr. Barry L. McAlpine. ©1994 Dr. Barry McAlpine.

Improving Your Life Every Day

Real people sharing real stories — for nineteen years. Now, Chicken Soup for the Soul has gone beyond the bookstore to become a world leader in life improvement. Through books, movies, DVDs, online resources and other partnerships, we bring hope, courage, inspiration and love to hundreds of millions of people around the world. Chicken Soup for the Soul's writers and readers belong to a one-of-a-kind global community, sharing advice, support, guidance, comfort, and knowledge.

Chicken Soup for the Soul stories have been translated into more than 40 languages and can be found in more than one hundred countries. Every day, millions of people experience a Chicken Soup for the Soul story in a book, magazine, newspaper or online. As we share our life experiences through these stories, we offer hope, comfort and inspiration to one another. The stories travel from person to person, and from country to country, helping to improve lives everywhere.

Share with Us

We all have had Chicken Soup for the Soul moments in our lives. If you would like to share your story or poem with millions of people around the world, go to chickensoup.com and click on "Submit Your Story." You may be able to help another reader, and become a published author at the same time. Some of our past contributors have launched writing and speaking careers from the publication of their stories in our books!

Our submission volume has been increasing steadily — the quality and quantity of your submissions has been fabulous. We only accept story submissions via our website. They are no longer accepted via mail or fax.

To contact us regarding other matters, please send us an e-mail through webmaster@chickensoupforthesoul.com, or fax or write us at:

Chicken Soup for the Soul
P.O. Box 700
Cos Cob, CT 06807-0700
Fax: 203-861-7194

One more note from your friends at Chicken Soup for the Soul: Occasionally, we receive an unsolicited book manuscript from one of our readers, and we would like to respectfully inform you that we do not accept unsolicited manuscripts and we must discard the ones that appear.

Chicken Soup for the Soul®

for the

The Power of Positive

101 Inspirational Stories about **Changing** Your **Life** through **Positive Thinking**

Jack Canfield,
Mark Victor Hansen,
and Amy Newmark

Attitude is everything. And this book will uplift and inspire readers with its 101 success stories about the power of positive thinking and how contributors changed their lives, solved problems, or overcame challenges through a positive attitude, counting their blessings, or other epiphanies.

978-1-61159-903-9

Chicken Soup for the Soul®

Think Positive

101 Inspirational Stories about Counting Your Blessings and Having a Positive Attitude

Jack Canfield,
Mark Victor Hansen & Amy Newmark
Foreword by Deborah Norville

Every cloud has a silver lining. Readers will be inspired by these 101 real-life stories from people just like them, taking a positive attitude to the ups and downs of life, and remembering to be grateful and count their blessings. This book continues Chicken Soup for the Soul's focus on inspiration and hope, and its stories of optimism and faith will encourage readers to stay positive during challenging times and in their everyday lives.

978-1-935096-56-6

Chicken Soup for the Soul®

Count Your Blessings

101 Stories of Gratitude, Fortitude, and Silver Linings

Jack Canfield,
Mark Victor Hansen, Amy Newmark,
Laura Robinson & Elizabeth Bryan

This uplifting book reminds readers of the blessings in their lives, despite financial stress, natural disasters, health scares and illnesses, housing challenges and family worries. This feel-good book is a great gift for New Year's or Easter, for someone going through a difficult time, or for Christmas. These stories of optimism, faith, and strength remind us of the simple pleasures of family, home, health, and inexpensive good times.

978-1-935096-42-9

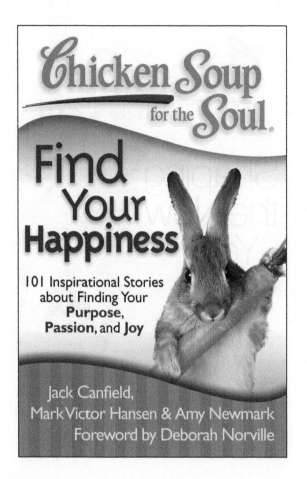

Chicken Soup for the Soul®

Find Your Happiness

101 Inspirational Stories about Finding Your **Purpose, Passion,** and **Joy**

Jack Canfield,
Mark Victor Hansen & Amy Newmark
Foreword by Deborah Norville

Others share how they found their passion, purpose, and joy in life in these 101 personal and exciting stories that are sure to encourage readers to find their own happiness. Stories in this collection will inspire readers to pursue their dreams, find their passion and seek joy in their life. This book continues Chicken Soup for the Soul's focus on inspiration and hope, reminding readers that they can find their own happiness.

978-1-935096-77-1

Chicken Soup for the Soul

Shaping the New You

101 Encouraging Stories about Dieting and Fitness... and Finding What Works for You

Jack Canfield,
Mark Victor Hansen & Amy Newmark
Foreword by Richard Simmons

No one likes to diet, but this book will encourage and inspire readers with its positive, practical, and purposeful stories of dieting and fitness. Readers will find hope, help, and hints on getting fit and staying healthy in these 101 stories from those who have been there, done that, and maintained it. Stories about wake-up calls and realizations, moving more and eating better, self-esteem and support, make this a great book for anyone starting fresh or needing a boost.

978-1-935096-57-3

Chicken Soup for the Soul

Inspirational Stories and Medical Advice for a Healthy You!

by DR. JEFF BROWN of
HARVARD MEDICAL SCHOOL

Think Positive
for
Great
Health

Use Your Mind to Promote Your
Own Healing and Wellness

Solid advice and transformative stories —
a true path to a positive outlook and great health!
~ Dr. Arthur J. Siegel

Inspiring Chicken Soup for the Soul stories and accessible leading-edge medical information from Dr. Jeff Brown of Harvard Medical School. Dr. Brown unlocks the mysteries of the mind/body connection and shows you how you can feel better and really be better by using your mind and thinking positively. The great stories will show you how other people have used positive thinking to affect their physical and mental well-being.

978-1-935096-90-0

www.chickensoup.com